William Francis Deverell

The Pilgrims and the Anglican Church

William Francis Deverell

The Pilgrims and the Anglican Church

ISBN/EAN: 9783337162382

Printed in Europe, USA, Canada, Australia, Japan

Cover: Foto ©ninafisch / pixelio.de

More available books at **www.hansebooks.com**

THE PILGRIMS AND THE ANGLICAN CHURCH

BY

WILLIAM DEVERELL

LONDON
REMINGTON & CO PUBLISHERS
HENRIETTA STREET COVENT GARDEN

1887
[*All Rights Reserved*]

PREFACE.

I HAVE been led to compile this short history of the Pilgrim Fathers by a strong desire to popularize amongst Englishmen the words and deeds of those illustrious plebeian countrymen of ours, which, although strange to most of us, are yet familiar to every schoolboy in America, and moreover form the brightest page in the brilliant annals of our imperial race.

My primary authorities are Mr. Bancroft's "History of the United States," Mr. Bacon's "Genesis of the New England Churches," and Dr. Robertson's "Colonization of America." The numerous quotations I have given are the touching words of the Pilgrims themselves, who have left the minutest records of their glorious enterprise, but they reach me mainly through the channels of Bacon and Bancroft.

I may say in reference to my original brochure on this subject that I have been honoured by more or less flattering communications from forty of our public men, including some of the most distinguished leaders, belonging to both political parties in the state. One other letter—which is, perhaps, the most laudatory—I have also received from the greatest living poet and man of letters of America. And I am at liberty to publish eight of those communications in application to the present work.

CONTENTS.

		PAGE
I.	Romanism	1
II.	Anglicanism	38
III.	Puritanism, or the Emancipation of England from Norman Domination ...	64
IV.	Restoration of the Norman Monarchy, Aristocracy, and Church	124
V.	Betrayal of England and the Norman Line into the hands of the Dutch Invaders, by the Nobility, Clergy, and Gentry ...	219
VI.	Despotism of the Nobility, Clergy, and Gentry under the Presidency of Dutch and German Puppet Kings	306

I.

ROMANISM.

We dwell with a pardonable natural vanity on the military and naval achievements of our race; our heroes' names and their fields of glory are as familiar in our mouths as household words; we are never weary of hearing how in the olden times our invincible archers swept every field and deck with their unerring cloth-yard shafts; how in these modern times nothing human could successfully withstand the bayonet-thrust of our terrible infantry; how every sea has resounded with the triumphant thunder of our gallant ships; how every nation has struck its flag to the irresistible logic of their broadsides; and, dazzled with the tinsel and glitter of these exploits, we are apt to forget that peace hath victories more glorious and enduring than war; that our race, by centuries of noble toil, has built up for us a monument of glory in the Western World, compared with which the renown of a thousand Cressys and Agincourts sink into absolute nothingness.

It is less than three centuries ago since the first British colonists set foot on American soil. A vast and unknown continent, peopled by the ferocious and treacherous Indian, lay before them, and behind them rolled the stormy Atlantic. With hearts as heroic as ever beat within human breasts, these unknown heroes turn their faces towards the setting sun, and commence that glorious march of civilization westward, which is the proudest achievement of our race—nay, I might say with truth, of the human race. The savage is forced back, the forest is cleared, the log-hut is reared, the crop is sown, the first settlement is planted, and from that moment England has been drained of her choicest spirits to recruit that noble army of toilers. Every tide has borne her best blood to the Western shores, and, wave on wave, her hosts of emigrants have surged ever onward, ever westward. And these hosts are ever marching with the measured British tread and the manly British speech, and they leave clear and unmistakable tracks behind them, broad as a continent; but not the ruined and devastated tracks of the warrior. No desolated country, no burning city, no blood-stained fortress, no battle-field piled with heaps of putrid dead mark their foot-steps. The primeval forest and the rolling prairie, dotted with the wigwam of the savage, are transformed by these heroes of toil into smiling corn-fields, studded with cosy hamlets and superb cities. The war-whoop of the Indian and the shriek of his victim give place to the shrill scream of the locomotive and the busy hum of commerce. Nature's laws are changed by them. These hosts of brave men, stout of heart and strong of arm, are marching not to the destruction, but to the creation of an empire. Myriads have fallen in that peaceful yet glorious strife, obscurely, but not in vain. The blood of these over-borne sons of toil has been the seed of a mighty nation—their triumph has been complete; for from the Atlantic to the Pacific they have marched victoriously, converting a vast continent from savagery to civilization, from heathenism to Christianity.

It is my intention, in my present work, to give as concise and as clear a description as possible of the settlement of our race on the continent of North America—an episode in the annals of the Anglican Church not unprofitable to contemplate at a time when that Institution is to be called upon not simply to explain and justify its *raison d'être*, but to render a rigid account of its stewardship. And I think it advisable to preface my subject with a brief geographical sketch of that portion of the continent (nearly the whole of it, by-the-bye) which is actually peopled by us, as I shall be then more clearly able to indicate, to localize as it were, the events I am about to narrate.

The United States, as we all know, consist at present of the whole central and most of the southern portion of North America. They lie between the 22nd and 49th parallels of north latitude and the 67th and 125th of west longitude. The surface of this vast country is estimated at 3,306,000 square miles. It is divided by nature into three sharply-defined sections. The Alleghany Mountains and the Atlantic bound in the eastern of these sections, and the Rocky Mountains and the Pacific the western. The Gulf of Mexico basin, including the valley of the Mississippi, forms the central section between these mountain ranges. British America, or the Dominion of Canada, as it is now called, lies to the north of the United States, and comprises an area of about 3,600,000 square miles. It embraces the whole breadth of the Continent, from the Atlantic to the Pacific, and stretches north to the Arctic Ocean. Its geographical features are simple. The eastern section consists of the valley of the St. Lawrence and its lakes, together with the northern end of the Atlantic slope; and the extreme western section, between the Pacific Ocean and the Rocky Mountains, forms a portion of what is called the Pacific slope. The east central section, if I may so term it, comprises the Hudson Bay basin, and the west central the valley of the Mackenzie and its lakes. The north-western peninsula of North America, hitherto known as Russian America, has become United States territory by purchase. It is a bleak and an inhospitable region of 500,000 square miles in extent, sparsely peopled by Esquimaux and Indians.

We thus find that the English-speaking race occupies on the North American continent upwards of 7,400,000 square miles of territory, equal to eighty-eight times the area of Great Britain; and my task will be to show how persecuted Puritans founded the Northern States of the Great Republic which forms the major portion of this vast territory, and which as a colony enabled us to conquer from the French the most important section of the region we now hold in the New World. And this subject naturally leads us, in the first instance, to a brief consideration of our various attempts at colonization prior to the landing of the Pilgrims.

The American continent was first discovered by the English. The expedition, fitted out under the auspices of Henry VII., and commanded by Sabastian Cabot, a native of Bristol, reached the mainland in 1497, some fourteen months before Columbus set foot on continental America. In the following year Cabot explored the greater portion of the eastern coast, and, on a subsequent voyage, Hudson's Bay and Strait. After these expeditions, however, the spirit of English maritime discovery languished. The Newfoundland fisheries had indeed at once assumed gigantic proportions; and our mariners, though bent on trade, naturally extended our geographical knowledge of the Western World; but from political and other causes, too numerous to particularize here, no expedition for American discovery sailed from our shores from Cabot's time till the reign of Elizabeth.

The death of Mary, the wife of Philip II. of Spain, snapped the ties which bound us to a country claiming exclusive possession of the New World, which ties had stifled the aspirations of hosts of adventurous English spirits, who thirsted for the fame and wealth which were to be acquired beyond the Atlantic. But the accession of Elizabeth (A.D. 1558), the representative, the embodiment, in fact, of the aspirations of her subjects, held out hopes of employment to those gallant men who were pining in forced inactivity. From her reign we date the commencement of a new and more glorious epoch of our history; and the nature of our subject will not permit us to pass by altogether unnoticed the queen who, in some sort, laid the foundations of our colonial empire, and whose name is still borne by the oldest and one of the noblest of our settlements. No true Englishman can mention with other feelings than those of pride and complacency the name of Anne Bullen's daughter, the great Queen Elizabeth. There is a sort of magic in the sound, which recalls to our memory the greatest and noblest men of our race—poets, warriors, statesmen, philosophers—who adorned that golden age of English genius, and who shed an imperishable lustre on the English name. And the "bright particular star" round which they moved was not, take her for all in all, unworthy of their homage. In spite of her faults, not to say her vices, there are few names in history of illustrious men that can compare with hers, and none of womankind. The noblest trait of her character was her unshaken patriotism, a virtue almost unknown among sovereigns. She was thoroughly national in blood, in heart, and in sentiment. She prided herself in her English descent; and though queen and head, she was at the same time part and parcel of the great English race, and gloried in the name of Englishwoman. She tells her people, when menaced with destruction by powerful enemies, "I know I have but the body of a weak and feeble woman, but I have the heart of a king, and of a King of England, too." And when standing on the threshold of eternity, broken in spirit and heart, she could address her people for the last time in these memorable words : " No queen will ever sit in my seat with more zeal for my country, or care for my subjects, nor any who will sooner with willingness venture her life for your good and safety than myself. For it is not my desire to live or reign longer than my life and reign shall be for your good; and though you have had, and may have, many princes more mighty and wise sitting in this State, yet you never had, nor shall have, any that will be more careful and loving." And it was this love of country, this pride of race which Elizabeth ever manifested, which won for her the hearts of her subjects in her own time, and which has embalmed her memory in the hearts of every succeeding generation of Englishmen. Her subjects felt, and the people of England still feel, that she was not simply queen of the English, but that she was in body, mind, and spirit, one of themselves.

Such was the character of this truly English queen, the patron, I had almost said the originator, of English maritime adventure and discovery. At her word of encouragement our dauntless mariners brave the countless dangers of Arctic-American exploration, and thread the intricate channels of the Atlantic and Pacific coasts, laying bare their hidden mysteries; at her command our invincible fleets sweep the enemy from every ocean; under her fostering care our hardy fishermen ply their peaceful calling on the banks of Newfoundland; and our gallant merchantmen already begin to whiten with their sails the remotest seas of the Old World. During her glorious reign Frobisher thrice explored the shores of Labrador and Greenland, in vain attempts to discover the north-west passage; and Drake, with like intent, coasted the western seaboard of North America. Sir Humphrey Gilbert lost his life on his homeward voyage from exploring the eastern coast, and his half-brother, Sir Walter Raleigh, wasted his fortune in the fruitless planting of our first and second colonies; the last of which perished miserably by famine or massacre. Yet, in spite of these disasters, or rather in consequence of them, the mind of England was being prepared for successful colonization. The returned settlers scattered broadcast through the land the most glowing descriptions of the climate, scenery, and soil of those enchanting regions which they had partially explored and planted, and which the Virgin Queen, in her enthusiasm, had named Virginia. Thus was instilled into the minds of sections of all classes of the community an ardent desire for American planting, which could not fail under favourable political circumstances to bear fruit.

A.D. 1606.—The set time was now fully come for laying on a sure basis, broad and deep, the foundations of our colonial empire. The accession of the Stuart dynasty to the throne of Great Britain, and the consequent cessation of hostilities with Spain, not only removed every obstacle from the path of those whose minds were predisposed to peaceful colonization, but threw out of employment hosts of warlike adventurers, who sought in the New World the fame and wealth which the Spanish war had so abundantly afforded them. This enthusiasm and greed of adventurers of all ranks of society, under the guidance and control of powerful corporations, led the way to the planting of Virginia, the nucleus round which were formed the various States of the late Southern Confederacy.

But New England, whose spirit and blood permeate and vivify the whole Northern population, had a far different origin. During the first half of the seventeenth century the relentless and cruel persecutions of the Anglican Church had forced from their homes a large section of the population of England, God-fearing men of whom this country was not worthy. These exiles—the first band of whom, with love and reverence Americans fondly call the Pilgrim Fathers—sought in the wilds of America that religious freedom which the Established Church denied them in their own country; and as this persecution gave birth virtually to the United States, it will be necessary to trace to its source that divergence of opinion in religious matters which led to such stupendous consequences.

And our first step to this investigation will be a rapid survey of the origin and development of Christianity.

The triumph of the powers of darkness culminated and seemed complete in that memorable scene on Calvary. The priests of Paganism remained the infallible teachers of mankind. The worshippers of Jupiter were still triumphant on earth. The Sun of Righteousness had set in blood, and darkness thick and palpable had supervened. Spiritual death would have again usurped the sceptre of the universe, but for a few fishermen of Galilee, who stood undaunted against a world in arms.

With hearts purged from every vice and inflamed with holy enthusiasm, the Apostles of Christ uplift the standard of the Cross, and, beneath its glorious folds, brave death under every hideous aspect. They fall martyrs of truth; but myriads of their disciples tread eagerly in their footsteps, emulous of the crown of martyrdom. Their combats and final victory are the most thrilling episodes in the annals of the human race. For three centuries these obscure and proscribed sectaries of Christ confront the pitiless storms of persecution; invincible in the might of weakness; victorious by right of suffering. In vain does the heathen world strive to drown Christianity in the blood of its votaries. Ten several times it plots the subversion of that faith against which the powers of man are of no avail; ten several times it bares its puny arm against the everlasting Church. It strikes, and at each blow the demon of persecution rears his ghastly head and stalks unfettered upon earth. His ravages are either partial or universal. Sometimes they embrace certain kingdoms and provinces only, at others they extend from Rome to the extremities of the world-wide empire; but all are marked with the same horrid characteristics. A brutal and pagan soldiery, united with brutal and pagan mobs, are let loose on the defenceless and outlawed Christians, and entire provinces are desolated by barbarities surpassing in atrocity those perpetrated by the Turks in the Bulgaria of to-day. Myriads are crucified, or burnt, or broken on the wheel, other myriads are devoured by wild beasts, or engulfed in raging seas. Every mode of death or torture, which cruelty could devise, was practised; no human or infernal agency was lacking to ensure the destruction of that which has been declared indestructible—the Church founded on a rock. So cruel and persistent was the Tenth and last Persecution, that in a single month eighteen thousand martyrs suffered death for Christ. The very enormity of the slaughter is its antidote; the blood of the saints quenches the fires of persecution, and ushers in the triumph of the Cross. Vanquished by its crimes, Paganism with its oracles, its sacrifices, and pageantry, disappears at the presence of its holocaust of victims. Henceforth the Church of Christ is supreme on earth.

And what was the character of those ecclesiastical organizations which thus subverted and supplanted the venerable superstitions of antiquity? Christ's own definition of a Church is the all-sufficient and conclusive answer: "Where two or three are gathered together in My name, there am I in the midst of them." And such was the origin and composition, subject to unlimited development, of all the primitive Churches. Determined, like the Apostle, to know nothing on earth save Jesus Christ, and Him crucified, and constrained by His love, the early converts, in assembling themselves together, and in constituting themselves into permanent associations for His worship, thought little, apparently, of that self-organization and self-administration of which they did not feel the pressing requirement; and their ecclesiastical polity, if so it may be called, was consequently the simple and natural outcome of their growth—the living expression of the will of a pure democracy, where all were brethren, acknowledging but "one Master, even Christ."

The government of these primitive organizations had, however, gradually developed, without Scriptural warrant it is true, into a non-political, and, therefore, an innoxious episcopacy. But the constitution of the Church had remained essentially democratic in character and principle, in spite of innovations arising from time and circumstance; for while the bishops and presbyters were the acknowledged leaders, their office and authority were derived directly or indirectly from the laity.

A.D. 324.—And such was the condition of ecclesiastical affairs when Constantine, from motives of policy, proclaimed the Christian religion the religion of the empire. That sagacious statesman, who had been an eyewitness of, and an actor in, the horrors of the Tenth Persecution, had become a partisan of the Christians after having been their persecutor. Although he was still a pagan, and to the last addicted to pagan practices, he regarded religion from a purely secular standpoint. And recognizing in the astounding growth of Christianity, in spite of the perpetration of every atrocity for its suppression, an earnest of its final triumph, he resolves to extend to it his protection, to perfect its organization, to consolidate and subsidize its hierarchy, and to enlist them in his service. He, therefore, established the Church, and endowed it with all the titles, honours, wealth and prestige of the pagan priesthood. The empire was divided into thirteen enormous dioceses, comprising one hundred and thirteen provinces, and each diocese was placed under the direction of a vicar. The general administration of the Church was entrusted to three, and subsequently to five, metropolitans, of co-equal power; their gradations of rank, however, being dependent on the political importance of their sees. The archbishops and bishops within the respective jurisdictions of these primates, who, from the commencement of the fifth century, were designated patriarchs, received from them their consecration, and were subject to their general supervision. But the absolute master of the Church was the Emperor. The highest dignitaries were his nominees, and received from him the pallium. Councils were convoked by his authority, and deliberated under his guidance and control. In becoming a Christian he had abdicated none of his imperial powers or dignities. He had but resigned the doomed title of Pontifex Maximus of an old and dying superstition, to become the supreme head and arbiter of a new and living faith. The Church from its inception was the instrument of its creator;

its servitude was the logical consequence of its political existence.

The hierarchy thus established was exalted as a sacred order above the laity, and invested, for political purposes, with vast ecclesiastical power. It perfected for the illiterate and wondering multitude a gorgeous and imposing ritual; it promulgated a creed binding on all Christians; it instituted a system of orthodoxy; and finally, pretending to be the sole depository of certain traditions of the apostles, it became, with the imperial sanction, in affairs purely ecclesiastical, the absolute master of the Church. And as the Eternal City was the political centre of the universe, its patriarch, in the natural course of things, was regarded as the supreme head. The Bishops of Rome had acquired, with universal assent, the primacy over all ecclesiastical dignitaries, and their title had been undisputed, until the transference of the seat of empire to Constantinople. Then, the new metropolis of the world, not satisfied with political pre-eminence, contended with ancient Rome for spiritual precedence. And this rivalry gave birth to the pious fraud on which the popes have founded their claim to ecclesiastical supremacy. It was now pretended that there had been a primacy among the apostles, of whom Peter was the prince; that he was the Vicar of Christ, the Rock on which the Church was to be built; and that to him had been entrusted the keys of the kingdom of heaven; and the power to bind and loose. St. Peter was now declared to have been the first bishop of Rome, and the popes were his legitimate successors. Yet it was in vain that the Apostolic See thus boldly asserted its divine right to supremacy, for its pretensions were never but temporarily recognized by its great rival. It is true that, from motives of policy, certain of the Eastern emperors had severally acknowledged the primacy of the Holy See, and that the Church of Constantinople had at their express command abandoned the claim it had persistently advanced to superiority over that of Rome; but these concessions and renunciations were not final. The eternal struggle was as often renewed and, surviving the disruption and destruction of the Roman empire, both Eastern and Western, it has been maintained under one form or another in every succeeding age, and subsists even to-day, as if practically to demonstrate the fallacy and monstrosity of the papal claim to universal supremacy.

Meanwhile the Church naturally shared the political vicissitudes of the State. And on the extinction of the Roman empire of the West (A.D. 476), the Gothic kings of course usurped the ecclesiastical as well as political rights of sovereignty which Constantine had transmitted to his successors. Nor did the destruction of the Gothic kingdom in Italy (A.D. 553) and the establishment of the Exarchate (A.D. 554) materially affect the political status of the Papacy. It is true, that Belisarius and Narses rescued Church and State alike from the barbarians' grasp and revived the might and prestige of the imperial name, but the Church remained in fetters. The deputies of the Eastern emperors were invested with ecclesiastical as well as civil and military powers. The exarchs or patricians of Ravenna, as they were indifferently styled, were the sovereigns of Rome, and as long as the power of the Eastern empire was unimpaired they exercised a complete control over the persons and government of the Sovereign Pontiffs. For example, Pope Vigilius having violated the conditions upon which he had been raised to the Papal chair, on the deposition and banishment of his predecessor, was arrested in the church of St. Cecilia, by command of the Empress Theodora, and conducted to Constantinople. In the imperial presence he was subjected to the grossest indignities and even to personal violence. Escaping from his persecutors, he fled to the church of St. Euphemia, but his pursuers having forced him from the pillars of the altar to which he was clinging, fastened a rope round his neck and dragged him ignominiously through the streets of the city until nightfall. He died at Syracuse on his release from a long and cruel imprisonment (A.D. 555). In a word, during a period of two hundred years, eighteen successive exarchs ruled with a rod of iron the Eternal City, when their power and authority were subverted by Astolphus, King of the Lomb.rds, who captured Ravenna and claimed the sovereignty of Rome as its dependency (A.D. 752).

The Roman Church now turns for succour and protection to the most warlike and powerful of those barbarous races, which, while conquering and reorganizing the Roman empire of the West, had themselves submitted to the yoke of Christ. Again, the Christian priest had conquered the conquerors of the world; and his second triumph, more glorious than the first, was a double victory, achieved at once over barbarians and pagans in the full tide of their military successes. The first and most illustrious of those spiritual victors—St. Remigius, Bishop of Rheims—confronts the terrible Clovis in his mad career of devastation and slaughter in Gaul, subdues his savage heart by the simple story of Christ's sufferings, and captivates his senses by the higher civilization he brings before his view. "Would that I had been there with my brave Franks!" bursts from the lips of the royal barbarian, as the eloquent prelate depicts the agony of the Crucifixion. With three thousand of his warriors the murderer of Soissons is received into the bosom of the Church amidst the pomp and splendour of a ceremonial which—even in the decay and dissolution of the empire—dazed and dazzled the rude conqueror. The sacred edifice was adorned with the richest tapestries, and redolent with the smoke of the choicest perfumes profusely burning in vases of gold and silver. "Father! is not this the kingdom of heaven where thou hast promised to lead me?" asked the wondering and tamed barbarian as St. Remigius, in full pontificals, led him by the hand towards the baptistery. "Bow thy head, Sicambrian!" said the bishop, "adore what thou hast hitherto burned—burn what thou hast hitherto adored!" Couriers soon carry the glad tidings of this triumph of the Catholic faith to Rome, and the delighted pontiff Anastatius hastens to felicitate the royal convert and proclaim him his glorious and illustrious son. At once the Gallic bishops and nation hail the papal champion and soldier as their deliverer from heretical domination, and with their powerful aid King Clovis makes an easy conquest of the Arian, and on the ruins of Latin Gaul founds the brilliant monarchy of France. To her old allies the Franks, then, the Church naturally appeals in the hour of danger for deliverance. And as a suppliant the pontiff Stephen visits Paris, crowns the usurper Pepin and his queen, and confers on him and on his sons the honours of the patriciate. Again the Franks become the champions of the Church, and twice (754-5) the redoubted Pepin scales the Alps, shatters the power of Astolphus, wrests from him the Exarchate, and bestows it in supreme and absolute sovereignty on the Papacy. But his son Charlemagne, as the ally of the Church, after annihilating the Lombard kingdom (A.D. 774) annexes Rome to his vast empire. The dignities and prerogatives of Constantine are revived in his person and family, and the Roman empire of the West is reconstructed in his honour. Hitherto Rome had acknowledged allegiance to the Eastern emperors, but on Christmas Day, in the year eight hundred, the Frankish conqueror, wearing the dress of a patrician, appears in the Cathedral of St. Peter, and after assisting at the celebration of mass, is kneeling at the high altar, when suddenly, amidst the acclamations of the multitude, Pope Leo III. throws over his shoulders a rich mantle of purple, crowns him Augustus and Emperor of the Romans, and pays him the homage which had been exacted by the ancient Cæsars.

Yet the hour of the complete political subjugation of the Church was also that of her greatest spiritual triumph. In Christianizing and civilizing the Franks, and in becoming their close ally, she had transformed those sturdy conquerors of the West into its invincible defenders against the countless hordes of their own barbarous and pagan countrymen; and thus, not only saved the Latin race and language, as well as the Latin civilization, from absolute annihilation, but enabled the conquered races, under the banner of Charlemagne, and in conjunction with their conquerors, to subjugate and evangelize the whole Germanic race. Moreover, she served as a bond of union and reconciliation between the Franks and Latins, and paved the way for the speedy and complete absorption—and utter extinction as a distinctive element—of the former into the bosom of the latter. And the modern Latin democracies, in their just irritation at the reactionary policy of the Church of Rome of to-day, should never be guilty of the base ingratitude of ignoring or repudiating the incalculable magnitude of the eternal obligations of their race to the early successors of St. Peter.

But the final dissolution of the empire of Charlemagne on the deposition of Charles the Fat (A.D. 888) inaugurates the most disgraceful and humiliating servitude of the Papacy. The oligarchy of Rome usurps the prerogatives of the emperors and robs the Church of the patrimonies which imperial munificence had bestowed. Abandoned women and licentious men contend for the sovereignty of the Holy See. The sword decides the pretensions of the rival factions, who desecrate with blood the holy places.

The tiara is worn by the vilest, weakest, or unhappiest of mankind. For twenty years the son of a prostitute governs the Eternal City. And so generally complete was the usurpation of the oligarchy, that the whole period of its triumph, extending over more than seventy years, may be regarded as a vacancy of the empire.

Weary at length of the tyranny of her domestic oppressors, the Church solicits the foreigner to come to her deliverance, and promises the imperial crown in exchange for St. Peter's patrimony. Descending the Alps with his German hordes, Otho the Great speedily conquers Italy (A.D. 962), subverts the power of the Roman oligarchy, frees the Pope, and grasps the diadem of the Western Cæsars. The Senate and people of Rome give to him and his successors for ever, the power of nominating popes, and of conferring investiture on bishops, and bind themselves, by solemn treaty, to prefer to the pontifical chair the imperial candidates. On the demise of the Pope, the envoys of Rome repair to the imperial court to receive from the Emperor the nomination of a successor. The monarchs of Germany bestow the Apostolic See, like that of an ordinary diocese of the empire, on their relatives, dependents, or creatures. The Church had but undergone a change of masters, domestic tyrants had given place to foreign conquerors, and Italian, in the majority of cases, to German Pontiffs.

As we have already seen, from the moment Constantine had established the Church, the popes had been the nominees and vassals successively of the Roman, Greek, Frank, and German emperors, and temporarily of the Gothic and Lombardic kings—nay, even of the aristocracy of Rome itself; and they had ordinarily made their spiritual influence over the masses subservient to the political aims and ambitions of their secular rulers. Yet the submission of the Church had always been conditional. The maintenance and exercise of the paramount authority of the imperial, royal, and oligarchical masters of the Papacy, had been at all times dependent on their ability to enforce their recognized rights with the sword.

A.D. 1072.—But the hour had now struck for the emancipation of the Church from secular control. Hildebrand (Pope Gregory VII.), the contemporary and admirer of our William the Conqueror, and in many salient features his ecclesiastical prototype, determined not simply to deprive the German emperors of the prerogative of nominating and confirming popes, but also to destroy every vestige of lay investiture, and to exalt the Papacy above all temporal powers. He would reduce into the domain of fact the pretensions which had been hitherto rather theoretically advanced than practically enforced by his predecessors. That the Church had been founded by God alone, and had ever been enlightened by His spirit; that the priesthood were His divinely-ordained ministers, and the popes were His Vicars on earth, were no new doctrines to the Church or Christendom; but Hildebrand, pushing them to their logical conseqences, boldly maintained that an authority thus emanating from the Supreme Being acquired a dignity surpassing all temporal grandeur, and possessed an inherent right to supremacy on earth. He compared the spiritual power to the glorious sun, the source of light and life; and the imperial power, the highest embodiment of the temporal, to the waning moon, his reflex. He determined to direct, control, and command in affairs secular, as completely and absolutely as in affairs ecclesiastical. He therefore emancipated the Church from the authority of princes by the abolition of lay investiture. He centralized the executive power of the Church by the transference of the electoral rights of the populace and priesthood of Rome to the College of Cardinals. He severed the last tie which bound the priest to the world by the rigid enforcement of celibacy; and from the Vatican he alone directed and controlled that vast army of priests of various race and tongue, who singly, or in masses, in their parishes or garrisoning those spiritual fortresses the monasteries, dominated with absolute sway the universal conscience of Latin Christendom. Thus did the carpenter's son of Soana, warring against imperial, royal, and aristocratic despotism, set his foot, as acknowledged conqueror, on the neck of crowned and brutal feudalism.

And this triumph of the Church was in a restricted sense a democratic triumph. In the secular world the masses groaned hopelessly beneath the iron yoke of an illiterate and turbulent chivalry, and were the perpetual and helpless victims of its foreign or domestic feuds. When knight met knight the courtesies of combat knew no limits; and the shock of arms, even in such battles as Tenchebray and Brenville, were almost innocent of bloodshed. But when the mail-clad bravo, mounted, and armed with brand or battle-axe of finest temper, hewed his facile way through reeling ranks of cowering serfs on foot, destitute alike of defensive armour and knightly weapons, he held not his hand till glutted and weary with human massacre. Of a truth the serfs had no will but their lords', no hope but in death. "Let us commend our souls to God," in sober earnestness they might have said, "for our bodies are the foe's." But within the pale of Holy Mother Church —the Republic of God—the omnipotence of blood ceased; the Vicars of Christ were indifferently patrician or plebeian. The democratic principle extinct elsewhere found here vitality and force. The swineherd of St. Albans, transformed into a priest, receives the homage of Germany's greatest emperor, and France's greatest king; and Frederic Barbarossa and Philip Augustus perform for Nicholas Breakspear the menial offices of grooms. Sprung from the people to a great extent, the priests were the natural champions and protectors of the poor, and the churches and monasteries were their places of refuge, and their store-houses amidst the turbulence and bloodshed which characterized those evil times. Moreover, the Church was an intellectual and cultured counterpoise to that incarnation of illiterate brute force, the feudal monarchies of the Dark Ages. The "Hercules without his club," as our first Plantagenet king cynically designated the Papacy, was the only earthly power that could restrain the unbridled licence and ferocity of feudal kings and peers, or materially alleviate the social miseries of the wretched populations subject to their yoke. Finally, as the sole depository of learning and official piety, the Church had been, since the overthrow of the Roman empire by the pagan hordes of the North, the intellectual and spiritual light of Western Europe without which mankind might have relapsed into barbarism, and the Latin race and language might have been smothered in blood.

Nevertheless, the general policy of the Papacy was animated by an ambition and a lust of power, in affairs temporal as well as spiritual, which aimed at universal empire. And the strange religious enthusiasm, which inflamed and hurled embattled Europe against the countless hordes of Asia, facilitated and hastened the triumph of this policy. The Crusades placed kings and peoples alike at the disposal of the Church. All were eager to enlist under her banners and obey her behests. The Fifth Crusade (A.D. 1204), indeed—which led to the conquest of Constantinople and the temporary subjugation of the Greek empire by the Latins—placed the whole Christian world at her feet. Yet the policy of the Papacy remained unchanged. Under her fostering care, ignorance and superstition everywhere reigned supreme. Her eternal watchward was still her material interests, and she hesitated at no atrocity in the suppression of whatever menaced them.

And how was this spiritual despotism maintained? What was the invariable line of conduct pursued by the Roman Catholic Church towards—shall I say for want of a better term—Dissenters, everywhere in Europe? We shall see.

The Papal hierarchy inaugurated their reign over the temporal powers by the burning of Arnold of Brescia and by a general persecution of the Waldenses. The immediate followers of Waldo in France were slain or dispersed, and the reformer himself died in exile, amid the mountains of Bohemia.

In France, in the thirteenth century, the Albigenses were exterminated. I have ever regarded this annihilation of the Albigenses as the blackest page in the black annals of Roman Catholic persecutions. A crusade is preached against these primitive saints of the Lord—the sons of the Holy Roman Church bear the cross of Christ stamped on their breasts, but the brand of murder is in their hands. Simon de Montfort, the father of our Earl of Leicester, and after him the Dauphin, afterwards Louis IX. of France, lead these crusaders on. The town of Bezières is about to be stormed, in which there are many Romanists, and Montfort demands of the Legate of the Pope, who accompanies his army, if these last shall be spared. The Legate answers: "Kill all, God will know His own!" Of a truth they did slay all, elsewhere as well as here; they ceased not until every true son of Languedoc lay weltering in his blood, and the fairest province of the sunny south of France became a waste and howling wilderness.

Two centuries later John Huss and Jerome of Prague suffered martyrdom at Constance, and the Reformation in Bohemia was mercilessly suppressed by the crusading armies of the Church. In the words of our Henry VIII., "They hunted it down like a wild beast, and driving it into a pit, they shut it up and kept it fast."

In the sixteenth century the Papal Church was stained with the culminating crime of Romanism, and in France this terrible scene was enacted. The Huguenots, goaded to madness by persecution, at length rise in arms, and, like brave Christian gentlemen as they are, hold their own against the hosts of the French King. Finding force of no avail, he resolves, by foul and midnight murder, to rid himself of God's freemen. A treaty of peace is concluded, which is to be cemented by the marriage of the King of Navarre, the leader of the Huguenots, and the King's sister, Margaret of Valois. The chiefs of the unsuspecting nobility and gentry are assembled in Paris to celebrate their prince's marriage; but at midnight after this marriage festival the bell of St. Germain l'Auxerrois tolls the death-knell of Protestantism; its peal is the preconcerted signal for a general massacre of the Huguenots of France, many the unsuspecting guests of their king. This king, Charles IX., and his mother, Catherine de Medicis, by his side, witness the massacre from the windows of the Louvre. The King has a fowling-piece in his hand, and ever and anon he fires into the crowd of fugitives that pass before his palace, fleeing from the knives of his assassins. The Duke of Guise—the cousin of Mary Queen of Scots—undertakes the assassination of the celebrated Admiral de Coligny, at the very house of his victim, and the good man dies in his bed-chamber beneath the swords of his assassins. Guise, from the court-yard beneath, "to make assurance doubly sure," calls to his bravoes to fling the body of Coligny to him. He kneels beside the corpse, and with his handkerchief wipes the stains of blood from that murdered face; he recognizes his enemy, and, spurning him with his foot, is satisfied. Thirty thousand Protestants are butchered on this and the following days in France. At the news there are rejoicings in Rome and Madrid, and by command of the Pope, Gregory XIII., a medal is struck to commemorate this glorious day of St. Bartholomew. But the living God neither slumbers nor sleeps; His avenging hand speedily reaches these persecutors. The King is on his death-bed. To his frenzied imagination, the spectres of his murdered subjects seize him and drag him to the tomb; he dies with shrieks of despair on his lips, and Guise, with many of his house, falls beneath the assassin's knife at Blois.

In the same century the Holy Inquisition had burnt out Protestantism in Spain; and the Protestants of Holland had been saved from extermination at the hands of the Spaniards, by their own strong arms and stout hearts, and by the aid of England.

Austria in the seventeenth century had again trodden out Protestantism in Bohemia, and the massacre of Magdeburg will enable us to form a passably accurate opinion as to her intentions in regard to Northern Germany had success favoured her arms.

In Piedmont, in the same century, a general massacre of the Vaudois took place. The mighty hand and stretched-out arm of God, through England, saved the remnant of this people. The threat of Cromwell to the Pope, "that the booming of English cannon should be heard at St. Angelo's," stayed these massacres.

Finally, and still in the same century, French Protestantism was practically exterminated by the Revocation of the Edict of Nantes. In 1685, the Huguenots of France, after undergoing a century of persecution—one day of which century I have already briefly alluded to—were expelled from their native soil, to the number of five hundred thousand souls, amidst the acclamations of their Roman Catholic fellow-countrymen, and that by the very monarch who has been pre-eminently designated " the Great."

Such were the antecedents of Romanism in all countries and in all ages. And by such atrocities as I have just described, she ever strove to extirpate Dissent, and so maintain intact her boundless powers and pretensions.

II.

ANGLICANISM.

A.D. 1071-1604.—In the meantime, England, which at the Norman Conquest had been the victim of papal policy, inflicted the first, and, in a political sense, the deadliest of a series of blows which have shattered the papal power in fragments, and laid the tiara in the dust.

The simple and primitive truths of Christianity, which Wickliffe had disseminated amongst the masses, could not have failed to impress deeply the minds of all sincerely devout and independent thinkers; and in the light of his teaching the mystifications and falsehoods which Romish priestcraft had interwoven with the plain Word of God must have become visible in all their naked deformity. People must have perceived at once that that Christianity which the Bible describes as so simple, that "they that run can read," and that "wayfaring men though fools shall not err therein," had been polluted, perverted, and corrupted, as soon as its teachers had assumed the proportions of an organized profession—as soon, in a word, as the Roman Church was established, and as an inevitable and natural consequence was swayed by the conflicting passions, ambitions, and interests which are, inherent to every large association of men, for whatsoever purpose incorporated. This institution, as we have already seen, had commenced its political career with being the pliant tool of governments, and had ended in being the master, protector, and abettor of that trades-union of monarchs, who have ever conspired against the liberties of mankind, of whom, in those dark ages, they were the tyrants and scourges, and whom they mercilessly ruled with the iron hand of the soldier and the superstitious lie of the Romish priest. But great as had been the moral blow dealt by Wickliffe to Romanism, and numerous as had been the converts to his views, we unfortunately owe our emancipation from its yoke to other causes. The changes in the constitution and government of the Church in England, which we call the Reformation, originated in the vilest passions of the worst of kings, in the licentiousness and greed of that monster who boasted "he had never spared man in his anger or woman in his lust."

Henry VIII. had been the great champion of Romanism. He had written with his own hand to the German princes, recommending them to deliver "Luther and his audacious treatises to the flames," unless he recanted, offering them at the same time his co-operation, and, if necessary, his life, for the accomplishment of so pious an object. Failing in this, he had combated with his pen that "Cerberus sprung from the depths of hell;" and the Pope, Clement VII., had rewarded his zeal by flattering the delighted monarch with the title of "Defender of the Faith." But in the course of time this fiery dialectitian had become weary of his wife, and had transferred his passions to a younger and more beautiful object. He now demanded of the Pope a dissolution of his marriage on religious grounds; his scruples of conscience, he pretended, would no longer allow him to cohabit with his brother's widow. The Holy Father was placed on the horns of a dilemma, or, to use his own homely phrase, "was betwixt the hammer and the anvil." He would have willingly obliged the King, even at the risk of destroying the Church's infallibility—a dispensation for the first marriage having been granted by Julius II.—but he was over-awed and overshadowed by the colossal power of Charles V., who vowed to defend his aunt, and who had the year previously given an earnest of the deadly quality of his vengeance by the storming and sacking of Rome, and the imprisonment of this very Pope for a less grave offence. The Holy Father therefore temporized, watching with eager eyes the progress of hostilities in Italy between Charles V. and Francis I., the ally of Henry; his mind ever inclining to this side or to that, with the various fluctuations of the contest. Threatened alike by both parties, he regulates his conduct by the irresistible logic of events. The star of Francis is in the ascendant, and everything is conceded to Henry; Charles is victorious, and every concession is revoked. Disgusted at length with this temporization, Henry lends a willing ear to Cromwell, who advises him to throw off the yoke of Rome, and declare himself supreme head of the Church in his own dominions. "Then," said Cromwell, "the clergy—sensible that their lives and fortunes are in the hands of their own monarch, hands which could be no longer paralyzed by alien interference from haughty antagonists — would instantly become the obsequious ministers of his will." This advice pleased the King, and was immediately acted upon, for Henry had at length resolved to reduce the Church—which William the Conqueror had established as a means of tightening his hold on England—to its original condition of absolute dependence on the Crown.

And here it will be necessary to consider for a moment the political circumstances under which the Norman Conqueror had created this Norman Church, with the avowed object of making it his servile instrument for enslaving the minds and souls of the Anglo-Saxon, Danish, and Celtic populations of this country, as he had already enslaved their bodies. King Harold and his brothers, with the flower of their race, had fallen on Senlac Hill, and a series of isolated and spasmodic revolts of the mixed races of Devonshire and the Welsh borders, the Celts of Cornwall, and the Anglo-Danes and Saxons of the Northern and Eastern counties, which had followed each other in rapid succession, had been repressed with the greatest barbarity. And by a winter campaign, attended with frightful sufferings to his troops, but culminating in the capture of Chester, he had crushed all armed resistance, and completed the conquest of the whole land. In his determination to render the Norman Conquest permanent—for he believed the clemency of Canute the Great had lost England to that conqueror's descendants—the Norman King was callous of human suffering, and deaf to the cries of mercy. He had literally converted into a desert—whitened with the bones of one hundred thousand of its inhabitants—the country lying between York and Durham, and had made of Hampshire a hunting-ground. Murder, conflagration, and famine had marked the track of his army everywhere; neither age nor sex was spared; all who crossed his path perished beneath the sword of this ruthless oppressor. Gradually the soil of England had been confiscated, and her princes and nobles, with one historic exception, had been either slain or disinherited, imprisoned or banished. Finally, Norman fortresses had sprung up, as if by magic, at every vital point, and—packed with Norman soldiers—dominated and overawed the ruined cities and ravaged country. And now the Conqueror has time to turn his whole attention to things spiritual. He had made up his mind to destroy the Anglo-Saxon Church of England, and create a new institution entirely devoted to his views. But with his habitual sagacity he effects this vast ecclesiastical revolution with the concurrence and support of the Apostolic See itself. At its outset—influenced no doubt by the Norman Conquerors of Southern Italy, who, after vanquishing, became the ardent champions of the Papacy, as well as by the general interest of the Roman Church—Pope Alexander II. had both encouraged and blessed his enterprise against England, sending him the banner of St. Peter, whose virtues would protect him against all dangers; therefore, the Norman Conqueror appealed with confidence to the old ally, who had displayed such zeal in favour of the invasion, to crown his holy work by undertaking the regulation of its spiritual concerns. And in response to his appeal—backed by their common friend the illustrious Lanfranc—his staunch allies Pope Alexander and great Hildebrand sent three legates into England on this important mission. These dignitaries—Cardinals John and Peter, and Hermenfroi, Bishop of Sion—the King retains about his person for the space of a whole year, treating them, in consideration of the mighty services he required of them, as if they were, says Ordericus Vitalis, angels of God. The famine-stricken land is mocked with the gorgeous ceremony and attendant festivities of a second coronation of the foreign king. Then, two Great Councils of all the Norman priests, and laymen, who had found rank and wealth in England, were in succession held, under the presidency of the Norman Conqueror, and Roman Cardinals, respectively at Winchester and Windsor. The Anglo-Saxon bishops and abbots, in a word the primate and all the higher clergy of the Church of England, were summoned, in the name, and by the authority of the Roman Church, to appear as criminals before this tribunal, and were, under various pretexts, degraded in a body, deprived of their sacred offices—which were conferred on Normans—and condemned to perpetual imprisonment in some particular fortress or monastery. The national clergy had everywhere to give place to the Norman, and the Saxon language to the French. Finally the celebrated Lanfranc, the beloved friend of both the Pope and King, was chosen primate of all England, and to him was intrusted the organization in all its details—subject to the general supervision of the Conqueror—of the new Norman Church of England, whose real and avowed mission it was to consolidate and perpetuate the Norman Conquest by making the Christian religion itself the means of enslaving the minds and souls of the conquered races of this land. And in every succeeding age, this Norman Church, in spite of its connection with the Papacy, was true to the traditions and interests of the conquering Norman caste, of which it was the offspring and spiritual representative; but by resisting the will of a monarch whose disposition was as despotic as the Conqueror's, she lost that partial independence which sprang from her union with the Roman Church, and was speedily reduced by Henry Tudor to that state of absolute dependence on the crown in which it had pleased the Norman Conqueror originally to place her.

A.D. 1531.—The Parliament without hesitation passed the necessary Acts required by Henry, conferring on him at the same time legislative power, which gave to his proclamations the force and authority of laws. The convocations, with one dissentient voice, readily acknowledged him as protector and supreme head of the Anglican Church; the prelates, clergy, and schoolmasters were commanded to preach and teach this new doctrine, and the sheriffs were to see that this duty was effectually performed. Finally, in order to give stability and perpetuity to this great and violent revolution, the vast lands and revenues of the ancient Church—including the fund which had been set apart for the maintenance of the poor, and which amounted to a third of the entire ecclesiastical wealth of the country—were confiscated, and handed over as a spoil to the aristocracy, whose support of these great changes was purchased and assured by the gratification of their insatiable cupidity.

Thus was the Pope dethroned in England, and the King usurped his functions; an English pontiff with unrestricted powers succeeded a foreign one; the capricious will of a tyrant became the only standard of religious faith; he could correct its errors, and enforce conformity to his views; henceforth the Anglican Church became, and has ever since remained, the absolute slave and emissary of the State, the natural enemy of the liberties of the people, of universal progress and enlightenment. It is true that Henry had emancipated himself from papal domination; but he rigidly and ruthlessly enforced every doctrine and right of the ancient Church. Protestants and Romanists were indiscriminately persecuted with unexampled barbarity. The former were burnt for refusing to subscribe to his confession of faith as enunciated in his "Bloody Statute;" the latter were hanged for rejecting his supremacy. He inaugurated a reign of terror unparalleled in its atrocity; a whole people were his victims, England was a vast aceldama.

A.D. 1547.—The death of this second founder of the Anglican Church emancipated England from a cruel bondage, and paved the way for the temporary completion of the Reformation. The Church had been split into two great factions ever since Henry had thrown off the papal yoke. The members of the one party, at the head of which was Cranmer, had been denominated the men of the new, and their opponents the men of the old learning. The former desired a complete severance from Rome, the latter hoped to effect a reunion with it. Both parties had been obliged to dissemble their own opinions, and accommodate themselves to the capricious will of their royal master; but at his death the reforming faction had gained the ascendency. The boy-king had been educated in the new faith; his uncle, the Protector, had been gorged with Church lands; the progress of this purely political Reformation, so far as it affected religion as an institution, was therefore inevitable. The first act of these *soi-disant* Reformers—many of whom were concealed Romanists, and all pledged to further innovation by the possession of Church property—was to complete the spoliation of that ancient institution by the seizure of the remainder of the abbey lands. They then swept away some of the most offensive of the old rites and ceremonies; and crowned their new edifice by the compilation of the Book of Common Prayer, which was substantially the same as the one now in use, and was but a garbled translation of the Roman mass-book. Finally, they denounced as heretics all who refused to acknowledge their pretensions, and enforced with arrogance and cruelty conformity to their views. Those bishops of the Romish faction who were too honest to dissemble, were at once dispossessed of their sees, and committed to prison; the revenue of their bishoprics becoming the plunder of the rapacious Reformers. The Princess Mary, tormented by her persecutors, made a vain attempt to escape to the Continent, and only secured liberty of conscience by the threat of her cousin, the Emperor Charles V., to declare hostilities. The masses were coerced to conformity to the new doctrines and liturgy by the martyrdom of the celebrated Joan Bocher and of George Van Parre, a Dutch physician resident in London.

Thus did the moiety of the members of a new institution, whose foundation had been laid in the lust, sacrilege, and atrocity of the prince of tyrants, suppress the rival faction, and arrogate for their Church a divine origin. With a far-seeing policy, they had preserved whatever of the old system was calculated to insure, to strengthen, and perpetuate their own ascendency; for they felt conscious that that perfect organization which had given to the popes for a thousand years an absolute dominion over the souls of mankind, could not fail, with able manipulation, to be equally serviceable to themselves. Therefore, under the new order of things, the King represented the Pope, and possessed all his awful attributes; the hierarchy remained intact, honours and wealth still giving weight and prestige to the bishops. The masses, systematically retained in ignorance, and, as a natural consequence, inclined to superstition, were still to a great extent dazzled and amazed by the splendours of a ritual that was incomprehensible to them. Not a single pretension of the ancient establishment did they waive or forego. They declared theirs to be the true and Apostolic Church, and by Act of Parliament asserted that their garbled liturgy had been framed by the direct inspiration of the Holy Spirit. Finally, forgetful that they owed their very existence to the sacrifice of their last vestiges of independence, and that they had ever proclaimed subserviency to their supreme temporal head as a divine obligation; forgetful that a monarch's breath had called them into existence, and that a monarch's breath could annihilate them—they conspired against their legitimate sovereign, and forfeited their heads as traitors before they were tried as heretics.

A.D. 1553.—On the accession of Mary a reaction was inevitable, for the Reformers had been her mother's and her own most bitter persecutors, and had even taken up arms to exclude her from the throne, branding her as illegitimate. The Romish faction of the Church at once obtained the ascendency. The ejected bishops were released from prison and restored to their sees. Once reassured as to the retention of their ecclesiastical plunder, the Parliament, who would, says the Venetian ambassador, "turn Turks or Jews at the command of their sovereign, but who would never restore the abbey lands," without hesitation repealed all the statutes which they had enacted against the old system during the two preceding reigns. The Roman Catholic Church was restored, papal supremacy was again acknowledged, and the legislature, bribed by the Emperor, unanimously decreed the enforcement of the ancient penalties against heretics. A large part of the clergy conformed; but those who were pledged to Protestantism by marriage, and who refused to abandon their wives, together with others who adhered to the new faith from conviction, fled to the Continent, where, however, many of them met with scant sympathy; for the foreign Reformers justly regarded them as political rather than religious exiles, and deemed their doctrines and system of Church government heretical. A moiety of the bishops likewise conformed, and there is no reason to doubt that others would have followed their example had they not been conscious that all concessions on their part would have availed them nothing, as they had rendered themselves personally obnoxious to the rival faction.

In spite of the isolated insurrections which stained with blood the reigns of the four last Tudor monarchs, and sprang directly or indirectly from religious causes, these repeated transitions in the religion of the State were effected with little opposition from the nation at large, who, if we are to judge by their generally passive and quiescent attitude, were more puzzled than enlightened at each transformation their Church underwent, as the Romish or the Reformed faction, in its turn, triumphed; or, to speak with correctness and precision, as the monarch, the absolute and acknowledged master of the national conscience and faith, chanced to be either Romanist or Protestant.

The extreme section of the Romish faction,

which had undergone a rigorous persecution during the preceding reign, now prepared to wreak on their adversaries a terrible revenge. They had, even as victims, regarded with scorn and derision the arrogant pretensions of their somewhat plebeian colleagues; it was, therefore, hardly to be expected that in the hour of triumph they would be merciful. Indeed, in their blindness and fury they resorted to the most atrocious measures of coercion, resolving with fire and faggot to extirpate heresy. But the calmness and fortitude with which the martyrs met death, under its most horrid aspect, shed an imperishable lustre on the Reformed faith, whilst it branded alike with eternal infamy those bishops and clergy of the Anglican Church who either actively compassed or passively consented to the destruction of their brethren.

A.D. 1558.—These barbarities ceased on the accession of Elizabeth, who at once rejected papal supremacy; not that she loved Rome less, but absolute power more. The new system—if system it might be called, which was but a travesty of the ceremonies, and a plagiarism of the ritual, of the ancient Church—was revived with still further concessions in favour of Romanists, by which the doctrine of transubstantiation and the practice of auricular confession were left to the independent judgment of the communicants, the acceptance or rejection of these articles of faith being conveniently regarded as immaterial. Acts of supremacy and uniformity were passed, and rigidly enforced. The bishops, who had by their cruelties in the preceding reign irretrievably committed themselves to Romanism, refused compliance with the new order of things, and were ejected from their sees; but the army of priests, with one hundred and seventy-five exceptions, conformed. The Queen, who did not abate one jot of the pretensions of her father, soon reduced the hierarchy to absolute submission to her will. The pretensions to infallibility of the old Church were, indeed, revived in favour of her institution, on purely political grounds; but its dignitaries, from the primate downwards, were treated with the indignity of menials whenever they dared in the slightest degree to question her omnipotence in the State ecclesiastical, or failed in immediate and unconditional compliance with her wishes in things temporal. But her thoroughly patriotic and dauntless spirit, the dazzling splendours of her reign, and the generally popular character of her government, reconciled the masses to the despotic authority of a Queen who had said, and in the main said truly, "I have always so behaved myself that under God I have placed my chiefest strength and safeguard in the loyal hearts and goodwill of my subjects."

A.D. 1603.—At her death "this royal throne of kings" was inherited by a pedant and buffoon, who was in character, in manners, and in person alike vile and contemptible. James had been bred in the Presbyterian faith, and had solemnly declared in the General Assembly at Edinburgh, with his "bonnet off, and his hands uplifted to heaven, that he praised God that he was born in the time of the light of the Gospel, and in such a place, as to be King of such a Church, the sincerest kirk in the world," and had, moreover, sworn as long as life should last to maintain the same in all its purity; adding, somewhat unnecessarily, "As for our neighbour Kirk of England, their service is an evil-said mass in English; they want nothing of the mass but the liftings."

But on his arrival in England, the fawning sycophancy and self-abasement of the bishops, the body as well as soul-enslaving tendency of their doctrines, and, above all, an identity of interests, had speedily effected his conversion to Anglicanism. He did not fail to perceive and appreciate the exquisite mechanism of an organization which, while servilely moulded upon the Roman pattern, retained all the political usefulness of its original without its sincerity and independence. He at once gave it his patronage and confidence, and secured its hierarchy in the possession of their honours and wealth, whilst they continued assiduously to preach and teach an absolute and a blind obedience to Royal authority in Church and State as a divine obligation incumbent on every subject; and not content with this, they desecrated the very Word of God itself with the most fulsome and impious flatteries of their royal master. These unholy leaguers then prepared to reassert and maintain the infallibility of their Church, and to mercilessly enforce uniformity.

But this was a task beyond their power, for it was absurd to suppose that honest and independent men, who had shaken off the venerable superstition of Rome, would for ever surrender their consciences and faith to the guidance of a new institution, which had been founded in the worst vices of our nature, and cemented with the blood of the saints. Indeed, from the earliest times when reform was preached, the mass of the thinking population, although prevented by the temporal power from holding aloof from that body, had not failed to condemn the purely political nature of its organization, to denounce as unscriptural and papistical the titles and dignities of its hierarchy, and to reject as idolatrous many of its doctrines and rites; and their numbers had now so greatly increased, that the persecuting and baffled Primate Whitgift, who had hanged Barrow, Greenwood, Penry, and other honourable and loyal men for refusing to conform, had said, "I have not been greatly quiet in my mind, the vipers are so many." These "vipers," or Puritans, as they were generally called, from their desire to restore Christianity to the purity and simplicity of apostolic times, had been the most eloquent, zealous, and indefatigable preachers of the Gospel among the masses; and we have it on the highest contemporary authority that the conversion of the nation at large to the new opinions was, under God, mainly, if not entirely, due to their herculean labours.

And when we reflect that in a material sense the confiscation of the vast domains of the ancient Church had been a calamity to all classes of the community save the highest, that the poor for whom the Church had ever amply provided—one-third of its revenues having been from time immemorial set apart exclusively for that sacred purpose—had been thereby thrown as a burden on the country, and that the spoliators of the Church and poor had been, in striking contrast with their clerical predecessors, harsh and rapacious landlords, ever sacrificing the rights and lives of their new tenants to their own insatiable avarice, it must be evident that Puritanic sincerity and enthusiasm, combined with Puritanic heroism and effort, could have alone triumphed over so many and such varied obstacles.

A.D. 1604.—The King, who had publicly declared with an oath that as he made the judges and the bishops, he made what he liked, law and Gospel, inaugurated his campaign against Puritanism at the mock conference at Hampton Court. Perceiving that his hierarchy were worsted in argument by their Puritanic opponents, he stood up the avowed champion of civil and religious despotism. Addressing the bishops, he solemnly declared that prelacy was the best, the indispensable support of his sovereignty. Turning towards the Puritans, he said, "You are aiming at a Scots' presbytery, which agrees with monarchy"—that is despotism in his acceptation of the word—"as well as God and the devil;" told them "that they wanted to strip Christ again, and bade them away with their snivelling." He concluded his harangue by declaring "he would make them conform, or harry them out of the land, or else worse," "only hang them, that's all." Then was witnessed one of the most humiliating spectacles of ecclesiastical depravity recorded in the black annals of Anglicanism. The King had scarcely ceased to speak when Bishop Bancroft, falling on his knees, exclaimed "that his heart melted for joy, and made haste to acknowledge to Almighty God His singular mercy in giving them such a king as since Christ's time had not been." And the aged but blood-stained Whitgift said, "Your Majesty speaks by the special assistance of God's Spirit." But Harrington, an eye-witness of this degrading scene, though a courtier and a partisan of the Church, writes, "I wist not what they mean, but the spirit was rather foul-mouthed."

And these were not mere idle words of King and prelates, but the deliberate expression of their fixed resolve to extirpate Dissent, and with it to extinguish " that precious spark of liberty which had been kindled, and was preserved by the Puritans alone." The Court of High Commission immediately resumed its horrid functions. This tribunal, which had been established for the discovery and suppression of Dissent, consisted of a body of forty-four clerical and lay commissioners presided over by the primate, and possessed an authority over the ecclesiastical affairs of the nation as absolute as it was iniquitous. Its victims were bound on oath to answer all interrogations incriminating others as well as themselves, and the highest contemporary authority assures us that " the inquisitors of Spain used not so many questions to trap their preys." The penalties inflicted were of the most atrocious character. Absence from church for a month was punished with fine and imprisonment; perpetual exile awaited all who did not recant and conform within three months after conviction; and a felon's death, without benefit of clergy, was the awful doom of those Puritans who either rejected these barbarous conditions or returned from banishment.

The Anglican Church now appeared triumphant everywhere. Episcopacy had been established in all parts of the British Isles; but for political rather than for religious purposes. In Ireland the revenues of the ancient and National Church had been transferred to the Anglican priesthood, but no attempt had been made to evangelize the population; the Irish benefices being in reality but political sinecures. The episcopal establishment in Wales, and the temporary one in Scotland, possessed the same characteristics. The Puritans alone resisted the absolute pretensions of Anglicanism, and maintained against it an unequal struggle for the civil and religious liberties of England.

Conscious of political power, and emboldened in their atrocities by impunity, the King and bishops dared to rekindle the baleful fires of Smithfield, and two victims perished in the flames ere the indignation of an outraged people could arrest the hands of the royal and prelatic assassins and save the martyrs at least from this most horrid form of death. But though denied the supreme gratification of burning its opponents, this Church —whose faith was ever conventional rather than real, and whose persecutions had ever a political rather than a religious tendency, and were therefore always cold-blooded—still continued its cruel work of repression, marking out as the especial object of its vengeance one of the most uncompromising and powerful of the nonconforming sects.

III.

PURITANISM,

OR THE EMANCIPATION OF ENGLAND FROM NORMAN DOMINATION.

A.D. 1604—1660.—Regarding the Scriptures as their only guide and authority in religious matters, the Independents claimed a complete emancipation of the mind and conscience from all ecclesiastical and secular control; and, as a natural consequence, rejected as anti-Christian the pretensions and titled hierarchy of the Anglican Church, which they, prodigal of their lives in the cause of truth, denounced as idolatrous in its doctrines, illegal in its ordination, and therefore invalid in its rites. They desired a complete severance of spiritual from temporal affairs, and maintained that each congregation constituted a complete and self-governing Church. They denied that the priesthood was a distinct order, conferring an indelible character; but, on the contrary, they affirmed that the voice of the brotherhood which ordained the priest could also unfrock him. Finally, with them originated the glorious doctrine of religious toleration, against which Anglicanism—subsidized by and necessarily a servant of the State—was bound in the nature of things to wage openly or secretly an eternal warfare.

The annihilation of the Independents was naturally the especial object of this Church's aim, to effect which it hesitated at no atrocity. The national voice had indeed constrained the reluctant prelates to quench the flames of persecution, but the halter, the glowing iron, the rack, and the shears were still busy at their horrid work. The courtier prelates, with their artificial faith and political aspirations, had still full licence to hang, brand, torture, and mutilate men "whose hearts the Lord had touched with heavenly zeal for His truth." Weary at length, and reeling in the terrible tempest, a remnant of "the poor persecuted flock of Christ," scattered over the rural and urban districts on the adjoining borders of Nottinghamshire, Lincolnshire, and Yorkshire, turned their despairing eyes towards Holland, "where, they heard, was freedom of religion for all men; as also how sundry, from London and other parts of the land, had been exiled and persecuted for the same cause and were gone thither." And these fugitives were but one small section of that glorious army of martyrs, who, "in the north parts," as in other places of the land, "had resolved," whatever it should cost them, "to shake off the yoke of anti-Christian bondage" which Anglicanism had imposed upon them. They were then called Separatists, from their determination to separate themselves, not simply from Anglicanism, and all other established politico-ecclesiastical organizations, which they denounced as alike corrupt, idolatrous, and anti-scriptural, but from the world at large, lying in wickedness. And their churches were so many voluntary and independent associations of Christians, who had "entered into covenant to walk with God, and one with another, in the enjoyment of the ordinances of God, according to the primitive pattern in the Word of God." But numerous as were these churches, and pitiless as was the persecution they all alike underwent, our attention must be limited, for sad and obvious reasons, to that heroic band of martyrs for whom so high a destiny was reserved; who had formed themselves, "as the Lord's free people," into a holy brotherhood (A.D. 1606), under the guidance of their pastor John Robinson, a man of fearless independence, at once tolerant and zealous in the cause of truth, and "worthily reverenced ... for the grace of God in him." The founder, host, and Ruling Elder of this famous Church was the venerated William Brewster. The son of a village postmaster of Nottinghamshire, he became the private secretary of Sir William Davison, whom he accompanied on an important and successful mission to the Netherlands; but on the unmerited disgrace of his distinguished patron he returned to his native place, and succeeded his father in his somewhat humble public office there. Deeply imbued with the religious fervour of Puritanism, he laboured for the extension of its glorious principles, "doing the best good he could, and walking according to the light he saw, till the Lord revealed further unto him." The Church at all convenient seasons assembled at his house, and long remembered in far distant lands with what "great love he entertained them when they came, making provision for them to his great charge." Among these humble worshippers was ever found a youthful yeoman from a neighbouring Yorkshire hamlet, who—left an orphan in his infancy, and reared by his paternal uncle—had joined the outlawed Church in opposition to the wishes of his friends. "To keep a good conscience, and walk in such a way as God has prescribed in His Word, is a thing which I shall prefer above you all, and above life itself," was his constant answer to all remonstrances. This was William Bradford, the future governor and chronicler of the first New England colony, and, with Brewster, the chief support and guide of that infant commonwealth. By self-instruction—like so many modern rulers of America—he became in after years a man of learning, capable of speaking French and Dutch, and reading Greek and Latin, while he studied Hebrew, "that he might see with his own eyes the ancient oracles of God in all their native beauty." Braving persecution for conscience' sake, this holy Church of simple husbandmen assembled on the Sabbath-Day, for upwards of a year, in the manor-house of Scrooby, the welcome guests of William Brewster, the Queen's "master of the posts."

And to Scrooby, then, that " mean townlet " on the river Idle, a few miles distant from its junction with the Trent, belongs the immortality of being the cradle of the " proper democracy," who, landing in America, founded New England, and moulded the civil and religious institutions of the Great Republic. Time has wrought changes in that classic spot sacred to the memory of the Pilgrim Fathers, where, all unconsciously, they were inscribing, in bright and shining characters, their lowly names upon the loftiest pinnacle of fame. The parish church of Scrooby still points its grey spire to the sky. The little river Idle slowly winds its way—through smiling cornfields, and green pastures stocked with grazing herds and bleating flocks—for ever onward to the Trent. But of the ancient manor-house, surrounded by its moat—now dry and partially filled up—nothing remains, save that portion of the venerable pile incorporated with the farm-house standing on its site. The memorials of the imperishable glory of the Pilgrim Fathers are found elsewhere. The New World is their fitting monument.

Their meetings in the manor-house of Scrooby soon drew down upon them the iron hand of persecution, which effectually stifled their common religious life, and closed for ever their conventicles in William Brewster's house. "Hunted and persecuted on every side," there was no resting-place in England for their feet. "Some were taken and clapped up in prison, others had their houses beset and watched night and day by apparitors and pursuivants, and hardly escaped their hands; and the most were fain to flee, and leave their houses and habitations and the means of their livelihood." In their dire extremity they sought in exile that personal security and freedom of conscience which Anglicanism denied them in the land of their fathers, and, "by a joint consent, they resolved to go into the Low Countries." No rash or inconsiderate step took they throughout the weary stages of their pilgrimage, for they ever followed a steadfast and infallible guide. "To go into a country they knew not but by hearsay, where they must learn a new language and get their livings they knew not how," seemed, they confessed, "an adventure almost desperate." "But these things did not dismay them, though they did sometimes trouble them, for their desires were set on the ways of God, and to enjoy His ordinances.

They rested on His providence, and knew whom they had believed." But our English Pharaohs, who, since the Norman Conquest, and under a religious mask, have in every succeeding age, and by virtue of hereditary descent, ruled, oppressed, and plundered the conquered populations of the British Isles—save when the proudly Celtic Henry Tudor checked, and Cromwell crushed them—refused to let God's people go that they might worship Him. Prelacy, their instrument and creature, was now no longer content simply to harry its victims out of the land. The ports were closed against the martyrs. " Though they could not stay, yet were they not suffered to go."

A.D. 1607. Their first attempt to escape from the persecuting fury of their adversaries was baffled by the treachery of the ship-master who had undertaken to convey them beyond the seas. Shrouded in darkness —for at dead of night alone could they hope to leave their native land, unhindered—they had, according to agreement, gone on board his vessel riding at anchor in the Wash, at no great distance from the port of Boston. They thought that they were free, when, suddenly, the myrmidons of the law—who had paid the captain to betray them—appearing upon the dismal and shameful scene, arrested them, and having rudely and indiscriminately searched and plundered the persons of their hapless victims, forced them into open boats, and took them again ashore. The next day the brutal captors led their innocent captives back into the town of Boston, "a spectacle and wonder to the multitude who came flocking on all sides to behold them;" and brought them before the magistrates. A dreary imprisonment as criminals awaited this first attempt of the Pilgrims to escape from England; but a second effort, six months later, although attended with heart-rending incidents, was more successful.

This time they told their strange, sad story to the Dutch captain and owner of a ship then lying at Hull, who agreed to take them over to his country. An unfrequented heath on the banks of the Humber, somewhere between Hull and Grimsby, was the appointed place of embarkation. The Scrooby Church reached that isolated rendezvous, "a good way distant from any town," a day too soon, the men going by land, and the women and children, with the household stuff, in a bark, which, as they were suffering from sea-sickness, was run into a neighbouring creek. The ship arrived next day to find that the ebb tide had left the little craft, with her passengers and freight, aground; and the skipper, to save time, sent in a boat for the men, who were sauntering about on shore. Brewster, Robinson, and Bradford, with the majority of their companions, had just reached the deck of the ship, and the boat was on the point of returning for the remainder of the men, when, to their dismay, they saw "a great company, both horse and foot, with bills and guns and other weapons"—it was the *posse comitatus*—rapidly approach the bark, and capture it. At once the captain, fearing for the safety of his ship, with a great Dutch oath, weighed anchor, and set sail, regardless of the sufferings of the departing and destitute exiles, who—thus suddenly separated from their companions and material resources—saw, on the slowly receding shores of their native land, their wives and children seized like the vilest criminals, and carried off to undergo the well-known horrors of common prison life. The few men left on shore dispersed and fled, save one or two, who undertook to render what chance countenance and comfort they were able to the unhappy captives.

"But pitiful it was to see the heavy case of these poor women—what weeping and crying on every side; some for their husbands who were carried away in the ship; others not knowing what should become of them and their little ones; others, again, melted in tears at seeing their poor little ones hanging about them, crying for fear and quaking with cold." But the captors were soon embarrassed by the magnitude of their success. "To imprison so many women and innocent children for no other cause (many of them) but that they must go with their husbands and fathers, seemed to be unreasonable, and all would cry out at them; and to send them home again was as difficult," for they "had no homes to go to." In the end, the magistrates contemptuously connived at their escape from England, being "glad to be rid of them at any price."

Meanwhile Brewster, Robinson, and Bradford, with their companions, were driven by a tempest to the coast of Norway, and narrowly escaped shipwreck. But in the moment of their greatest peril, "when man's hope and help failed, the Lord's power and mercy appeared," as they believed, in answer to their prayers, "and He filled their afflicted minds with such comforts as everyone cannot understand." This two days' voyage took them a stormy fortnight, and left, at least on William Bradford's mind, vivid and life-long recollections.

A.D. 1608.—They landed at Amsterdam, where the whole Scrooby Church soon followed them, and they "met together again with no small rejoicing." But they felt conscious it was not their abiding dwelling-place. "They knew they were Pilgrims, and looked not much on those things, but lifted up their eyes to heaven, their dearest country, and quieted their spirits." The following year they removed to Leyden, which was the last stage of their wanderings in Europe, and their resting-place for nearly twelve years. The story of their lives in this hive of industry is soon told. These hardy English husbandmen, transformed, with rare exceptions, into handicraftsmen, soon "saw," says Bradford, "the grim and grisly face of poverty coming upon them like an armed man, with whom they must buckle and encounter, and from whom they could not fly. But they were armed with faith and patience against him; and though they were sometimes foiled, yet, by God's assistance, they prevailed and got the victory." And in spite of "hard and continual labour," they enjoyed "much sweet and delightful society and spiritual comfort together in the ways of God. . . . so that they grew in knowledge and other gifts and graces of the spirit of God, and lived together in peace and love and holiness." Meanwhile, by reason of the persecutions they had endured, their consequent flight with its strange and pathetic incidents, and their Christian walk and conversation under all circumstances, "their cause became famous," and "many came to them from different parts of England, so that they grew a great congregation." Their pastor, the "learned, polished, and modest" Robinson, a man "not easily to be paralleled," defended in able and elaborate works their discipline and polity against antagonists not less known than Bishop Hall, of Norwich; and at the University of Leyden he even enhanced that reputation for scholarship which had won for him the highest honours Cambridge had to bestow. The controversy which Arminius and Gomarus, the late professors of theology at Leyden, had bequeathed to the schools, was naturally maintained with exceptional vigour at their own university; and, about this time, the learned Episcopius, the

Arminian professor of theology there, promulgated a series of theses, challenging to public disputation all opponents. The Calvinistic professor of theology and the clergy of the city feared to encounter a man whose renown for erudition has descended to our own times. But, at their pressing instance, Robinson stood forth the champion of orthodoxy, and on three several occasions, "before great and public audiences," the Pilgrims assert that "the truth had a famous victory," and that Robinson silenced, or to use their own words, "put to an apparent nonplus," his formidable antagonist.

But notwithstanding the liberty of conscience which Holland afforded them, the Pilgrims were "restless" until they could realize their desire to again "live under the protection of England, and that their children after them should retain the language and the name of Englishmen." Thus biassed, in the course of time, circumstances, with "sundry weighty and solid reasons" which they have left on record, inclined them to remove to some other place. At home they "had only been used to a plain country life, and the innocent trade of husbandry," but in Holland, where they had resolved to continue to live together as an organized social and religious community, they were constrained to learn and practise, as they best could, mechanical occupations. Many who came to them from England left them weeping, "unable to endure the great labour and hard fare, with other inconveniences, which they underwent, and were contented with. . . . Yea, some preferred and chose the prisons in England rather than liberty in Holland with these afflictions." Their numbers were being thinned by death, and they, imbued with all an Englishman's pride of race and love of country, deemed themselves but exiles in a strange land, and dreaded abruption by an alien race. "Many of their children, sharing their parents' burdens, bowed under the weight, and became decrepit, the vigour of manhood being consumed, as it were, in the bud. But that which was more lamentable, and of all sorrows most heavy to be borne, was that many others, by these occasions, and the great licentiousness of youth in that country, and the manifold temptations of the place, were drawn away by evil examples into extravagant and dangerous courses. . . . Some became soldiers, others took upon them far voyages by sea, and some others worse courses, tending to dissoluteness and the danger of their souls." But, perhaps, the strongest reason for the resumption of their pilgrimage was "a great hope and inward zeal they had of laying some good foundation (or, at least, to make some way thereunto) of propagating and advancing the Gospel of the kingdom of Christ in these remote parts of the world; yea, though they should be but the stepping stones unto others for the performance of so great a work." Moreover, persuaded that they constituted a community, founded and regulated after the pattern, and animated with the spirit of the Churches of the apostolic times, they were naturally anxious to perpetuate a system of ecclesiastical government which embodied the germ of all liberty, civil as well as religious. To men thus circumstanced, the whole earth afforded but one sure place of refuge, and the Pilgrims' thoughts persistently and naturally wandered westward. Not thoughtlessly or recklessly did they enter on this great and perilous enterprise. "We verily believe and trust," said they, "the Lord is with us, to whom and to whose service we have given ourselves in many trials: and that He will graciously prosper our endeavours according to the simplicity of our hearts therein. We are well weaned from the delicate milk of our mother-country, and inured to the difficulties of a strange land; the people are, for the body of them, industrious and frugal, we think we may safely say, as any company of people in the world. We are knit together as a body in a most strict and sacred bond and covenant of the Lord, of the violation of which we make great conscience, and by virtue whereof we hold ourselves straitly tied to all care of each other's good and of the whole. It is not with us as with men whom small things can discourage. . . . Yea, though we should lose our lives in this action, yet may we have comfort in the same, and our endeavours will be honourable."

After protracted negotiations with the King, and a certain corporate body, the Pilgrims, without a royal charter, or any valid grant of land, prepared to depart. A minority of the more youthful and resolute had elected to be the pioneers of the rest, and they were to be conducted by the governing elder, William Brewster (the host of the Church when it had worshipped in secret in the manor-house of Scrooby), a man of wide and varied experience in affairs, an able though modest teacher, and their most distinguished *confrère*. All things being now ready, a solemn fast was proclaimed, and the Pilgrims assembled together at the house of their pastor, which was also their church. "Let us humble ourselves before our God, and seek of Him a right way for us, and for our children, and for our substance," was the subject of his valedictory address. And his words of loving and sagacious counsel never faded from their memory. Then, "the brethren that stayed at Leyden," writes one of the Pilgrims, "having again solemnly sought the Lord, with us, and for us, feasted us that were to go, at our pastor's house, being large, where we refreshed ourselves, after our tears, with singing of Psalms, making joyful melody in our hearts, as well as with the voice, there being many of the congregation very expert in music, and, indeed, it was the sweetest melody that ever mine ears heard."

The "wholesome counsel" of Robinson to the Church was temperate, evangelical, and catholic, to a degree almost unknown in that age, and possessed a pathos and solemnity inseparable from the occasion.

"We are ere long to part asunder; and whether ever I shall live to see your faces again is known to the Lord. But whether the Lord hath appointed it or not, I charge you, before God and His blessed angels, that you follow me no further than you have seen me follow the Lord Jesus Christ. The Lord has more truth and light yet to break forth out of His holy Word. I cannot sufficiently bewail the condition of the Reformed Churches, who are come to a period in religion, and will go no further than the instruments of their reformation. Luther and Calvin were great and shining lights in their times, yet God did not reveal His whole will to them, and were they now living they would be as ready and willing to embrace further light as that they had received. I beseech you to remember it—it is an article of your Church covenant, that you be ready to receive whatever light or truth shall be made known to you from the written Word. But I exhort you to take heed what you receive for truth, and well to examine and compare it, and weigh it with other Scripture of truth before you receive it. For it is not possible the Christian world should come so lately out of such thick anti-Christian darkness, and full perfection of knowledge break forth at once."

A.D. 1620.—The day of embarkation having

now arrived, Brewster and his companions, accompanied by the whole congregation, repaired to Delft-Haven, where the *Speedwell* awaited them. The departure was a memorable and pathetic spectacle. "After prayers," writes Edward Winslow, "after prayers performed by our pastor, when a flood of tears was poured out, the brethren that stayed at Leyden accompanied us to the ship, but were not able to speak one to another for the abundance of sorrow to part." And for the last time the united Scrooby Church—the exiles who had gone on shipboard, and their friends who thronged the shore—with heads uncovered, knelt around their spiritual and civil guide and teacher, who hitherto had led them in their wanderings, and had brought them, inseparably one in aim and sentiment, to the threshold of the mighty enterprise for which he trained them. In tones which thrilled with and inspired emotion, John Robinson, with confidence, commended the departing Pilgrims to the holy keeping of Him who holds the seas in the hollow of His hand. He ceases, and rough sailor hands and voices perform their part in this world-moving drama, of which alone our English common people, hitherto unknown as an independent and controlling force in history, were the immortal actors. Unlashed from her moorings, the *Speedwell* spreads her white sails to the breeze, and firing a farewell salute to Robinson—whose face they never more beheld—and to the remnant of the Scrooby Church left on Dutch soil, the Pilgrim Fathers commence their famous voyage, amidst the sympathetic tears of even Dutch spectators. "We gave them," says Winslow, "a volley of small shot and three pieces of ordnance; and so, lifting up our hands to each other, and our hearts for each other to the Lord our God, we departed and found His presence with us."

The first place of their destination was Southampton, where they were joined by the *Mayflower* and a few friends recruited from various parts of England. There they received an official letter from their pastor, who had been unwillingly detained at Leyden by the entreaties of the majority of the congregation, who remained there, and by urgent private affairs. A public meeting of the Pilgrims was probably convened on board the *Mayflower* to hear their ruling elder, William Brewster, read this most interesting and important document, which demands attention not simply on account of its own intrinsic merits and its influence on the minds and actions of the future founders of New England—for we are expressly told it "had good acceptàtion with all, and after-fruit with many"—but as the first historic and official utterance of the Scrooby Church preparing to transform itself into a "body politic." In language eloquent from its simplicity and transparent sincerity, Robinson assures his departing flock: "I do heartily, and in the Lord, salute you, as being those with whom I am present in my best affections and most earnest longings after you, though I be constrained for a while to be bodily absent from you. I say 'constrained,' God knowing how willingly, and much rather than otherwise, I would have borne my part with you in this first brunt, were I not by strong necessity held back for the present. Make account of me, in the meanwhile, as of a man divided in myself with great pain, and as (natural bonds set aside) having my better part with you. And though I doubt not but in your godly wisdom you both foresee and resolve upon that which concerneth your present state and condition both severally and jointly, yet I have thought it but my duty to add some further spur of provocation to them that run well already—if not because you need it, yet because I owe it in love and duty." He next, with deepest love and sympathy, admonishes them to cultivate—as vital to the stability of "the house of God, which you are, and are to be"—(*a*) heavenly peace with God and their own consciences; (*b*) peace among themselves, and (*c*) individual and collective unity of purpose for the general good. He then proceeds: "Lastly, whereas you are to become a body politic, using among yourselves civil government, and are not furnished with any persons of special eminency above the rest to be chosen by you into office of government, let your wisdom and godliness appear not only in choosing such persons as do entirely love and will diligently promote the common good, but also in yielding unto them all due honour and obedience in their lawful administrations; not beholding in them the ordinariness of their persons, but God's ordinance for your good; nor being like the foolish multitude, who honour more the gay coat than either the virtuous mind of the man or the glorious ordinance of the Lord. But you know better things, and that the image of the Lord's power and authority, which the magistrate beareth, is honourable in how mean persons soever. And this duty you may both the more willingly and ought the more conscionably to perform, because you are, at least for the present, to have only them for your ordinary governors, which you yourselves shall make choice of for that work. Sundry other things of importance I could put you in mind of, and of those before mentioned in more words. But I will not so far wrong your godly minds as to think you heedless of these things, there being also divers among you so well able to admonish both themselves and others of what concerneth them." And prayerfully and confidently John Robinson commits his flock to the guidance and protection of " Him in whom you trust, and in whom I rest . . . whose providence is over all His works, and especially over all His dear children for good." Under such holy auspices did the Pilgrims turn their faces towards the west, having, like our first parents, a new world

"all before them, where to choose
Their place of rest, and Providence their guide."

In a fortnight the *Mayflower* and the *Speedwell* drop down Southhampton Water—with less fanfaronnade but greater import than the armaments of our Edwards and our

Henries, bound for the shores of France—and soon reach the high seas; but they put back for repairs into the port of Dartmouth, where they are detained for another fortnight. Again they sail, but when a hundred leagues from Land's End, the leakiness of the *Speedwell,* and the timidity of the captain and his companions, force them to return, this time, to Plymouth. Here the smaller vessel is discharged, and Robert Cushman, with a few others, left behind, and the *Mayflower* alone, taking on board the whole of the Pilgrims, numbering one hundred men, women, and children, finally sets sail from Plymouth on the 6th of September, 1620. They were bound for the banks of the Hudson, where they intended planting their colony, but, after a long and stormy voyage, were conducted, by stress of weather, to Cape Cod, one of the bleakest and most sterile points on the coast. It was impossible, however, to prosecute any researches for a more desirable haven; for the winter was at hand, the Pilgrims were wasted by sickness, their supplies were almost exhausted, and the ship had been hired simply for the voyage across the Atlantic.

But before landing they regulated by

solemn compact their system of civil government, which was purely democratical. The whole body of men formed a supreme legislative assembly, which was the depository of all power, and by whom the executive, consisting of a governor and assistants, were to be elected annually. In affixing their signatures to that famous instrument which constituted them "a civil body politic," and which solemnly bound them "to enact, constitute, and frame such just and equal laws, ordinances, acts, constitutions, and offices, from time to time, as shall be thought most convenient for the general good of the colony," the Pilgrims happily revindicated for all time the inalienable right of mankind to primitive freedom and self-government. "This," says Bancroft, "was the birth of popular constitutional liberty. In the cabin of the *Mayflower* humanity recovered its rights, and instituted government on the basis of 'equal laws' for the 'general good.'" Their first act of sovereignty was the immediate and unanimous election of John Carver, "a man godly and well approved among them," as governor for the year.

Winter was at hand, and the greatest haste

was demanded in the selection of a place of settlement; but the shallop, on which depended the sole hope of successful exploration, was found to be so frail that seventeen days were required to make it fit for service. Meanwhile, the more energetic of the Pilgrims, restless at enforced inactivity, made a painful exploration by land. Except a heap of maize, they found nothing but Indian graves. They returned alike unsuccessful from their first expedition in the shallop wearied with plodding over steep hills and deep valleys covered with snow.

Affairs looked almost desperate, but the Pilgrims never faltered, and at length (Dec. 6) the shallop was ready to depart on her final voyage of discovery. The crew consisted of ten Pilgrims and a like number of seamen. The pilot was the mate of the *Mayflower*. He assured the Pilgrims of the existence of a good harbour, which he had visited in a previous voyage, on the opposite shores of the bay. They set sail in weather so foul that they could not stretch directly across the bay, and so cold that their clothes, steeped in the dashing and freezing spray, were like coats of iron. On their third day of unsuccessful exploration, they coast the western shores of the bay, the pilot assuring them that they will reach a good harbour before nightfall. But towards evening, a north-east wind, which gradually freshens to a gale, and is accompanied with snow and rain, assails the frail bark. In the fierce shock the rudder breaks, the mast is shivered into fragments, the sail falls overboard, and darkness is settling down on the wild waste of waters. "Yet, by God's mercy, they recovered themselves," and the flood-tide carries them towards the shore. Doubling a headland, they are borne into a cove full of breakers. "The Lord be merciful to us!" cries the affrighted pilot, "my eyes never saw this place before," and in his infatuation he would have run the boat ashore. "About with her," shouts a seaman, who is painfully steering the boat with an oar, "or we are cast away." The order is promptly obeyed; they row for their lives out of the jaws of death; and cheered by the voice of the sturdy seaman, they pull lustily ahead, until they reach a fair sound, and find shelter under the lee of a rising ground. They land in darkness and a deluge of rain; but after midnight the wind shifted to the north-west, and it froze hard. And kindling a fire, they wished for the day.

When morning dawned, they found they were on a small island, at the entrance of a good harbour. And in a few days the *Mayflower* cast anchor in the bay. With a patriotism which neither persecution nor exile could abate, they named both harbour and settlement after the last English ground their feet had pressed. The Pilgrims landed on Plymouth Rock, that was

"to their feet as a doorstep
Into a world unknown—the corner-stone of a nation!"

Their famous voyage ended, as it had begun, in prayer. "Being thus arrived in a good harbour, and brought safe to land, they fell upon their knees and blessed the God of heaven who had brought them over the vast and furious ocean, and delivered them from all the perils and miseries thereof, again to set their feet on the firm and stable earth, their proper element."

"As they landed," says Bancroft, "their institutions were already perfected. Democratic liberty and independent Christian worship at once existed in America. The consequences of that day are constantly unfolding themselves as time advances. It was the origin of New England; it was the planting of New England institutions. Inquisitive historians have loved to mark every vestige of the Pilgrims; poets of the purest minds have commemorated their virtues; the noblest genius has been called into existence to display their merits worthily, and to trace the consequence of their daring enterprise."

But glorious as is the retrospect of the landing of the Pilgrims, viewed in the light of its stupendous consequences, the reality was cheerless, dark, and tragical. It was midwinter in a climate far more rigorous than the one to which they had been accustomed. As their boats neared the shore the shallowness of the water compelled them to leap into the waves and wade to land. The barren soil was wrapped in a covering of snow to the depth of several inches. Infected with mortal diseases, and destitute of adequate supplies of provisions, the Pilgrims, amidst frost and snow, toiled wearily to construct places of shelter in that waste wilderness. One by one, overborne by sickness and toil, they sank peacefully to rest. The survivors, wasted with disease, were incapable of taking care of the dying. Before the return of spring the governor and one-half of the colony had ceased to exist. But never, in the hour of direst extremity, did the forefathers repine, or abate one jot of hope or confidence. Enjoying a free worship of God and His Christ, which was the object of their exile and their all in all, they with cheerful and quiet minds confronted all eventualities; death for them had lost its sting, and life its intense bitterness.

"God had sifted three kingdoms to find the wheat for this planting,
Then had sifted the wheat, as the living seed of a nation;
So say the chronicles old, and such is the faith of the people."

But the news of this great mortality pierced the heart of Robinson their pastor, who wrote: "The death of so many, our dear friends and brethren, oh! how grievous hath it been to you to bear, and to us to take knowledge of; which if it could be mended with lamenting, could not sufficiently be bewailed. But we must go unto them, and they shall not return unto us." Yet he manfully reminds them: "In a battle it is not looked for but that divers should die; it is thought well for a side if it get the victory, though with the loss of divers, if not too many or too great."

On the approach of genial weather this excessive mortality ceased; but famine, with its attendant horrors, and the savage, with his barbarities, remained to be vanquished. The latter danger appearing the more urgent, the Pilgrims were constrained at once to assume a military organization, and to nominate a commander. Their choice fell on Miles Standish, in many respects the most eminent man of the community. He was a Low Country veteran, of great courage and experience, and the reputed descendant of that Standish who gave Wat Tyler his *coup-de-grâce*. Although no member of the Church he revered, he " had chosen with the people of God to suffer affliction," and he proved the sword and shield of the infant Commonwealth. The natives were easily conciliated or repressed, for their numbers had been thinned by a fearful pestilence which three or four years previously had swept over the north-eastern sea-board with such deadly effect that the tribes in the immediate vicinity of the colony had been almost entirely annihilated.

A.D. 1621.—A somewhat dramatic incident signalized the commencement of the intercourse of the rival races. One day in early spring (March 16th)—the weather was "warm and fair," and "the birds sang in the woods most pleasantly"—as the surviving

Pilgrims were assembled in the "common house" to mature their plans of defence, they were startled by the appearance of a savage, who, boldly entering the village, marched "straight to the rendezvous." As he approached he exclaimed, "Welcome, Englishmen!" and would have entered their rude council-chamber had not the Pilgrim chiefs prudently forbidden the unknown savage to thus inspect their scanty numbers and weak condition. He bade them possess the soil of Patuxet, on which they had founded their new settlement, to which, he said, there was no Indian claim, the aborigines having, with a solitary exception, perished in the late epidemic. This was Samoset, a Wampanoag, who had learned a little English of the fishermen frequenting what is now the coast of Maire. As the first Indian with whom they had been able to communicate, Samoset was naturally to the Pilgrims an object of great interest and close scrutiny. They have minutely described him as a tall, straight, beardless man, with long black hair, cut short in front, whose only covering was a leathern girdle, fringed to a span's breadth or thereabouts, and only arms a bow and two arrows, one of which was headless. He possessed the native dignity of his race, and was free of speech so far as he could find utterance in English. The Pilgrims "questioned him of many things" and "he discoursed of the whole country, and of every province, and of the Sagamores, and of their number of men and strength," saying that he was himself a Sagamore from the eastern coast. He further told them that the Nausites, who attacked their exploring party, had killed three Englishmen some months before, and that they were incited to those hostile acts by the kidnapping raids upon their coast of a seafaring ruffian of our race. To screen him from the bleak March wind which had begun to rise, they "cast a horseman's coat about him," and having feasted him, longed for his departure. But, as he persisted in remaining with them until morning, they lodged him for that night, and watched him.

Two days later Samoset brought with him five messengers from Massasoit, the great Sachem of the tribe on their southern border, and within a week four others. With these last came Squanto, the sole surviving native of Patuxet, who—kidnapped with nineteen others of his tribe seven years before—had been sold to slavery in Spain, and thence had found his way to London, where he had "dwelt in Cornhill with Master John Slainie," a merchant interested in the New England fisheries. Sent back by Slainie as an interpreter, the Indian at this juncture had returned to his native village, to find its site and corn-fields occupied by strangers.

By means of Samoset and Squanto the Pilgrims entered into immediate negotiations with Massasoit, who occupied with all his men the summit of a neighbouring hill. And Winslow having placed himself in the hands of the Indians as a hostage, King Massasoit and twenty of his warriors repaired to Plymouth. There, Governor Carver and Elder Brewster, with Bradford, Allerton, and Captain Standish—the freely-chosen leaders of the Pilgrims—met in solemn conference their tall, lithe Indian guests, painted according to their fancy in gay or sombre colours, clad in the skins of wild beasts, and distinguished by the long black hair, the weird, yet elegant features, and majestic bearing of their race. Our democratic English exiles anticipated, by more than sixty years, Penn's justly vaunted treaty with the Indians. And that universal sentiment of honour, which prompted and pervaded the minutest actions of the wonderful and stainless lives of the Pilgrims, was but the natural and spontaneous outcome of the deathless religious principles they had professed in good report and evil, "whatever it should cost them," and "that it cost them something" this history hath declared. In simple verity, these lowly husbandmen and artisans—despised and exiled by our Ruling Caste—were the embodiment, in human flesh and blood, of the ideal knights, whom poets of all nations, and all ages, have fondly feigned and sung. The painted savage of the wilderness, with whom they came in personal contact, felt and owned, as if by instinct, the potent influence of their commanding virtues. At once, an offensive and defensive alliance was concluded between the high contracting powers; which remained inviolate for more than fifty years; and a treaty of commerce cemented the amicable relations of the confederate races. Moreover, Massasoit undertook to communicate to the neighbouring tribes and nations the details of this sacred compact, and to offer to include them also in the conditions of the peace. This was the first imperial act of democratic England, in the mighty drama which made the New World ours.

A.D. 1622.—But Canonicus, the Sachem of the powerful Narragansets, whose numbers were estimated at thirty thousand, and whose territory embraced the dimensions of a modern state, was hostile to the Pilgrims. A messenger of his brought into Plymouth a bundle of new arrows, wrapped in the skin of a rattlesnake, as his gage of battle. A council of war was held, and, after a brief consultation, Governor Bradford—the successor of John Carver—"stuffed the skin with powder and shot, and sent it back, returning no less defiance to Canonicus, assuring him that if he had shipping now present thereby to send his men to Narraganset, they would not need to come so far by land to us; yet withal showing that they should never come unwelcomed or unlooked for." It was a bloodless victory. The terrified barbarian at once sought relations of amity with a people possessing such strange and deadly weapons of war.

But, notwithstanding their proud defiance of the Narraganset King, his threats revealed to the Pilgrim chiefs, not simply the weakness of the military defences of the colony, but the necessity of converting that weakness into strength. The site of Plymouth was a stretch of rising ground, embracing a hill of considerable elevation, whose summit commanded a view of land and sea perhaps unrivalled for extent and beauty on the whole Atlantic coast. The village was, roughly speaking, cruciform, and in its centre stood the Governor's house, in front of which—probably before the arrival of the hostile messenger of Canonicus—a battery of four guns was planted in a square enclosure, so as to sweep the crossing streets in all four directions. But within six weeks of the departure of the Indian envoy, the incessant and united labour of its inhabitants had surrounded Plymouth with a formidable stockade, strengthened at convenient points with flankers, and pierced with three gates, which were locked at night and guarded, a watch being also set when needed in the daytime. And one or two months later they completed their fortifications, by constructing upon the hill a large square fort of solid timber, with a flat roof and battlements, on which they mounted a battery of six guns, and kept a sentinel on constant watch and ward. This structure was at once the meeting-house and citadel of the exiled Scrooby Church.

The Pilgrims had, at the same time, to

grapple with their more formidable adversary, famine. The struggle was long and arduous. The arrival in autumn of brethren destitute of provisions reduced them to the brink of starvation. For months they had absolutely no corn, fish and water being their only nourishment. In their hour of greatest need they were rescued from death by generous succour from fishermen in the offing. Not until after the third harvest was the old colony exempt from general scarcity of food. This happy change in their condition was facilitated by the abandonment of the system of community of goods, which had hitherto prevailed, and had depressed the energies of the industrious, whilst it had encouraged the indolence of the listless and improvident. Land was now allotted to families in proportion to their numbers, and the incentive of personal interest soon produced the most satisfactory results. Prosperity flowed in upon the colony. The growth of corn soon exceeded the consumption, and became one of the chief staples of trade. A friendly intercourse sprang up with the surrounding natives, many of whose chiefs voluntarily acknowledged the supremacy of the colonists, or were overawed by them; and a lucrative commerce in skins and furs seemed to offer a tardy but material compensation for the sufferings and labours of the past.

But the brightening prospects of the colony only served to arouse the cupidity of London merchants, who sought to monopolize the gains of a trade which the energy of the Pilgrims had created. With this object in view, sixty needy adventurers arrived out, who, after forcing themselves on the hospitality of the Pilgrims for several months, settled at Weymouth, in Boston harbour. Devoid of industry and foresight, they were soon reduced to a famishing condition; and relied chiefly for subsistence on the supplies they could wring from the natives. Harassed by exactions, and infuriated by oppression, the Indians silently formed an atrocious scheme for a sudden and universal massacre of the whites. The allied tribes delayed to strike only until their plans were so perfected that their blow should fall with fatal effect. But Massasoit, the benevolent chief, with whom the Pilgrims had entered into an alliance for mutual defence, touched by the arrival of an embassy of condolence from the colonists during a dangerous malady, and grateful for the care and "confection" of

Winslow, which had restored him to health, revealed to his allies the details of this horrid plot, and thus saved them from impending ruin.

Promptitude and vigour characterized the conduct of the Pilgrims in this supreme crisis of their career. "Though it much grieved us," writes Winslow, "to shed the blood of those whose good we ever intended and aimed at as a principal object in all our proceedings," yet "we knew no means to deliver our countrymen and preserve ourselves save by returning the mischievous and cruel purposes" of the savages "upon their own heads, and causing them to fall into the same pit they had digged for others." To ensure secrecy and dispatch the town meeting or legislative assembly of Plymouth—which was then in session—authorized Governor Bradford, Assistant Allerton, and Captain Standish to undertake the general management of the war. And this committee of public safety entrusted the direction of military operations to Standish, with unlimited powers. But his instructions were precise touching the arch-conspirator in the atrocious plot—the Sachem Wattawamat of the Massachusetts—who had already wantonly imbrued his hands in the blood of the whites. The captain was directed to forbear to strike, "if it were possible, till he could make sure of that bloody and bold villain, whose head he had order to bring with him, that he might be a warning and terror to all of that disposition."

A.D. 1623.—The chivalry of Plymouth, under the undaunted Standish, hastened to the rescue of their erring countrymen. The victory they achieved was decisive. Pecksuot, an Indian chief of gigantic stature, fell in single combat, stabbed to the heart by the Puritan captain. His death was the signal of battle. In emulation of their chief the Pilgrim warriors spring forward, seize and slay with their own weapons, which they wrench from them, the ringleaders of the diabolical plot whom Massasoit had named. As their champion fell, the war-whoop of the savages rang through the forest, whence were poured flights of feathery arrows into the slowly advancing Puritan line. But a few deadly volleys of musketry scattered the affrighted savages, who fled, hotly pursued, into the depths of the wilderness, reckless of the fate of the brave Wattawamat, who had fallen pierced through the brain by a musket ball. Thus did Standish rid the

Pilgrims of their would-be assassins, and inscribe the first battle and victory on the records of the Great Republic. Some of the intruders, who owed their lives to the gallantry of the Pilgrims, remained with them, the others returned home.

"Bravely the stalwart Miles Standish was scouring the land with his forces,
Waxing valiant in fight, and defeating the alien armies,
Till his name had become a sound of fear to the nations."

From the crest of the great hill she crowned as with a glorious diadem, Plymouth could now look down in peace and safety upon the broad ocean and broader continent which lay on either hand at her feet.

But the intelligence of this necessary bloodshed grieved the gentle heart of Robinson, who was pining in enforced exile at Leyden. "Concerning the killing," he writes, "of those poor Indians, of which we heard at first by report, and since by more certain relation. Oh! how happy a thing had it been if you had converted some before you had killed any! Besides, where blood is once begun to be shed, it is seldom stanched for a long time after. You will say they deserved it. I grant it; but upon what provocations and invitements by those heathenish Christians? Besides, you being no magistrates over them, were to consider not what they deserved, but what you were by necessity constrained to inflict. Necessity of this, especially of killing so many (and many more, it seems, they would if they could), I see not. Methinks one or two principals should have been full enough, according to that approved rule, 'the punishment of the few, and the fear to the many.' Upon this occasion let me be bold to exhort you seriously to consider the disposition of your captain, whom I love, and am persuaded the Lord in great mercy and for much good hath sent you him, if you use him aright. He is a man humble and meek among you, and toward all, in ordinary course. But now, if this be merely from a human" (he means unregenerate) "spirit, there is cause to fear that, by occasion especially of provocation, there may be wanting that tenderness of the life of man, made after God's image, which is meet. It is also a thing more glorious in men's eyes than pleasing in God's or convenient for Christians, to be a terror to poor barbarous people, and, indeed, I am afraid, lest by these occasions, others should be drawn to affect a kind of ruffling course in the world."

Yet, the Church which landed from the *Mayflower,* and stood alone amid a continent of savage nations, must be the Church Militant *par excellence* on earth, or cease to exist. And the large square fort of the Pilgrims, which served the double purpose of church and fortress, was a fit emblem of their condition. But the victories of Standish soon gave stability to the infant Commonwealth. Slowly, but surely, it now commenced its onward, ever-progressive march to greatness, dotting its settlements to the very banks of the Connecticut. The remainder of the Church at Leyden, with the wife and children of Robinson, removed to America, but the patriarch himself died ere he could see the promised land. "But," says Bancroft, "his heart was in America, where his memory will never die."

Thus did the Pilgrims, the victims of persecution but never persecutors, plant the first democratic Commonwealth on American soil, and present to posterity the unique and glorious spectacle of a state cradled in freedom, untainted from its inception by that spiritual and temporal servitude which had been hitherto the hereditary curse of the masses of mankind in every recorded age. Not blindly did they accomplish their high destiny. Conscious of great achievement in having placed present freedom and prospective empire within the grasp of their persecuted compatriots, they could proudly exclaim: "As one small candle may light a thousand, so the light here kindled hath shone to many, yea, in some sort to our whole nation." And loving friends in England could cheer them, in the midst of their greatest sufferings, with the prospect—nay, the certainty—of a coming immortality of glory in this world and the next. "Go on, good friends," write they, "comfortably; pluck up your hearts cheerfully, and quit yourselves like men in all your difficulties, that—notwithstanding all displeasure and threats of men—the work may go on which you are about, and which is so much for the glory of God and the furtherance of our countrymen, as that a man may, with more comfort, expend his life in it, than live the life of a Methuselah in wasting the plenty of a tilled land, or eating the fruit of a grown tree. . . . Let it not be grievous to you that you have been instruments to break the ice for others who come after with less difficulty. The honour will be yours to the world's end." And we—who share their blood—recognizing all the marvellous consequences which have flowed from their heroic enterprise, as the natural and inevitable outcome of the triumph of the immortal principles of Puritanism, regard the beacon of liberty they kindled " on the wild New England shore" as

> ". . . . le phare immense
> D'un nouveau monde et d'un monde trop vieux ; "

the dazzling source of the hope and confidence of all who long and wait for the political and religious emancipation of the human race.

Thus did those sturdy husbandmen of Lincoln, Nottingham, and York—emerging from the black obscurity which had hitherto so dismally enshrouded their fellows of all countries and all ages—proudly take their places in the pages of universal history as emphatically the noblest, most illustrious, and important band of personages who have ever influenced for good the destinies of mankind. And thus did they enshrine therein their marvellous adventure, as incomparably the greatest and best event of which this world has ever been the theatre. And while the princes, peers, and priests who have enslaved the wretched

populations of the Old World, behold with
silent fear and wonder their puny states
eclipsed by the Pilgrims' Great Republic of
the new, the toiling millions of the earth
acclaim its English democratic founders as
par excellence the true, the heaven-born kings
of men. Uncrowned kings sprung from the
ranks of the people, who dwarfed and set in
their right light the ghastly and bloody
achievements of the crowned despots of all
time, when landing on Plymouth Rock they
took possession—in the name of the God of
peace and liberty—of the New World, which
He had predestined and prepared as the glorious and unparalleled heritage of the democracy of England freeing themselves by
expatriation from Norman domination in their
native land.

After the expulsion of the Pilgrims from
their native land, the Anglican Church continued its war of extermination against all the
Puritanic sects with unabated violence and
ferocity. " Nothing," says Milton, " nothing
but the wide ocean and the savage deserts of
America could hide and shelter them from
the fury of the bishops." A glorious army of
martyrs, numbering twenty-one thousand two
hundred souls—the best and purest in England

—were thus driven into exile. An embryo nation migrated to the western wilds. There they founded the Northern States of the Great Republic, and moulded its civil and religious institutions on the broad and indestructible basis of free Christian worship, universal education, and popular sovereignty. Their descendants number to-day one-third of the entire white population of the United States; and, since the conquest of the south, have formed the governing element of the whole country. Such has been the grand *rôle*, in the history of mankind, of the descendants of the victims of the Anglican Church; their power, magnificence, and all-reaching influence in the immediate future, are inconceivable in their immensity.

We have given the testimony of America to the unblemished and peerless renown of the Pilgrims; but England, in spite of Carlyle's eulogy, has been false to their memory. Our history is replete with descriptions of butcheries by sea and land, which, beyond a wasteful and wanton shedding of human blood, were in the vast majority of cases attended with results of the most ephemeral nature, or with absolutely no results at all; but it passes silently by, or at the utmost notices with a few brief sentences the peaceful yet glorious triumphs of the Pilgrims; triumphs teeming with consequences as indestructible as the universe itself. The man, *du gentilhommerie*, be he genius or fool, whose good fortune it has been for a single day to lead our army or fleet to battle, is embalmed in our history, and his memory is honoured by us all. Nay, to descend still lower. Let us approach that epoch which lacked the proud and exultant patriotism of the Commonwealth, and which ignored the dictum of the Puritan Sea-King, that the paramount duty of Englishmen is to prevent the foreigner from fooling us. Since 1688, when, by an act of sublime treachery, the aristocracy, with the assistance of a Dutch army, dethroned the last of the Stuart kings and usurped his power, we have bent the knee to a succession of alien princes, whose connection with this country has alone redeemed them from merited oblivion. Conscious that it would be impossible to govern England under an avowedly oligarchical *régime*, and too mutually jealous to elect a monarch from their own ranks, the governing families transferred the crown to obscure strangers, who, having no legitimate right to any "golden round," were naturally content to play a subordinate, an ignoble *rôle*. And rearing aloft these mockery kings as symbols of royalty only, they, with affected *empressement*, have paid homage to the work of their own hands, and by their example have made a conventional kind of loyalty to the foreigner fashionable. Content with the substance, they have left the shadow of power to their German *protégés*, and have governed England absolutely in their name, until the late parliamentary changes shook to its foundation, if it did not annihilate, the political edifice they had so elaborately constructed. The system subverted, there remains only the keystone of that system, the German princeling element, which, being no longer of use to its whilom masters, must ultimately sink into the obscurity whence a caste has raised it. In a word, for the past century and a half, the Wettins of Saxe-Coburg-Gotha—whose salient characteristic is an elasticity of conscience in religious matters, which transforms those Lutherans into Romanists in Belgium and Portugal, Greek Catholics in Russia, and Anglicans in this country—the Wettins of Saxe-Coburg-Gotha, together with others of the same genus, have been the princes and monarchs of

> "This royal throne of kings, this sceptred isle,
>   This earth of majesty, this seat of Mars,
>   This other Eden, demi-paradise."

And not content with this unparalleled exaltation, the aspiring blood of the Wettins, insatiate of honours, mounts still higher, and with the powerful patronage of Benjamin Disraeli attains its wildest aspirations. That blind worshipper of our German Court, imbued with oriental notions of royalty natural to his race, but repugnant to our own, laboured to surround with a sham splendour the German offspring of our Act of Settlement, and to transform those ghosts of monarchs into the solid substance of English kings. And in pursuance of his inflated and fantastic policy, the highest pinnacle of earthly grandeur must be theirs. This mediatized ducal family from the depths of Germany, the representative of one of the pettiest of its lilliputian principalities, must forsooth in England don the purple and fill the primal seat of Orient. Therefore, in spite of England's protest, and in violation of her historic conscience, India, the fairest, mightiest and most famous realm of Asia—to conquer and reorganize which a hundred years of British genius, valour, and blood were required—was transformed into an empire; the gorgeous and imperial throne of Tamerlane and Akbar was reconstructed; and the glittering but gory diadem of the Grand Moguls was, with surpassing meanness, snatched from the bayonets of our soldiers who sustained it with their life-blood, for the glorification of our new family of the Wettins of Saxe-Coburg-Gotha. In a word we have, *bon gré mal gré*, bestowed both royal and imperial rank upon these German princelings; we have waged long and bloody wars in defence of their interests and the interests of their country; and sacrificing one Continent to their latent despotic instincts, we have replaced it with another, and have called its nascent English empires by their names. Nay more, England has been their stalking-horse to power in other lands, and has planted or upheld them on the thrones of foreign states. But Robinson and Carver, Brewster and Bradford, Winslow and Standish, Cushman and Allerton, those truly illustrious men *sans peur et sans reproche*, the founders of the freest and mightiest state on earth—compared with which, within a century, the entire German empire will be as nothing—are forgotten in the land of their fathers. Their very memory is dead in England, on which they have shed an imperishable lustre whose glory and tongue they have perpetuated for ever.

And the prelates, who thus decimated the Puritans by death and by proscription, were the nominees and parasites of the infamous Buckingham and his licentious mother; by whom simony had been reduced to a system, and presentations to all holy offices had been regulated on a purely commercial ratio where lust did not intervene. These prelates were the slaves and emissaries of a corrupt Court, whose tentatives at a *rapprochement* with Rome had been rejected by the Papacy with scorn and derision. Devoid alike of faith, of principle, of patriotism, they were the most powerful because the most insidious champions of secular despotism. Spurned by Rome, they assumed the garb and *rôle* of Rome in England, and on behalf of their royal master they sedulously preached the doctrine of passive obedience to, and non-resistance of, the powers that be, as a Divine ordination, and strove to keep the weak-minded and ignorant classes in subjection by the dread of the eternal punishments they boldly and unblushingly denounced against all who dared resist their tyrant, whom they styled the Lord's anointed. These men, infuriated at the escape of the Puritans, procured the suspension of emigration, and the appointment of a commission for the government of the American plantations. The primate and his associates were invested with absolute ecclesiastical and secular powers; but ere they could stretch out their hand against the Puritans their Church was involved in ruin. Striving for universal domination over the national conscience of the British Isles, they attempted to impose on the Scots the garbled translation of the Popish missal which they call their glorious liturgy; and by so doing evoked a tempest of popular indignation which was not allayed till Anglicanism and kingly tyranny—those twin monsters which have ever gone hand-in-hand together, save on one memorable occasion—perished in the blood of Laud and Charles, their incarnation and essence.

The destruction of the ancient system of government was consummated by the fall of the House of Peers and the landed gentry, and was signalized by the public execution of the Duke of Hamilton and Lords Holland, Derby, and Capel, of Sir George Lisle and Sir Charles Lucas. The fire and smoke of Marston Moor and Naseby had consumed the Norman Monarchy, Church, and Baronage, which, at the Conquest, had deprived the people of their liberties, and stripped them of their lands; and which had governed them in every succeeding age as conquerors and masters: and on the ruins of the unexampled slavery founded by William the Bastard and his followers, and perpetuated by their descendants, at length arose the stately structure of national sovereignty. Yet the overthrow of the conquering Norman Caste had been hastened and facilitated by their own internal dissensions and divisions. From their own ranks had sprung the early leaders of the Revolution; but as the struggle progressed and widened in its scope, the armed and disciplined multitude threw aside the Essexes, the Manchesters, and the Fairfaxes, and, marching from victory to victory, finally subdued the proud descendants of our Norman conquerors, and broke from the neck of England the servile yoke which had been imposed upon her on the battle-field of Hastings. And the famous Long Parliament, purged of its anti-national elements, had legalized what the military prowess of Cromwell and his Ironsides had accomplished, by the formal abolition of the old and the institution of the new order of things. "Be it declared," ran the memorable decree which founded the Republic, "be it declared and enacted by this present Parliament, and by the authority of the same, that the people of England, and of all the dominions thereunto belonging, are, and shall be, and are hereby constituted, made, established, and confirmed to be a Commonwealth or Free State: and shall be henceforth governed as a Commonwealth and Free State, by the supreme authority of this nation, the representatives of the people in Parliament, and by such as they shall appoint and constitute officers and ministers under them, for the good of the people, and without any King or House of Lords." The Anglican Church, as we have seen, had been already utterly destroyed.

"In things of the mind," Cromwell had written to Speaker Lenthall seven years before the commencement of his Protectorate, "in things of the mind, we look for no compulsion, but that of light and reason."

And the chief corner-stone of his policy was freedom of conscience in the broadest acceptation of the phrase. He had destroyed kingly tyranny with the sword, and subverting that extraordinary system of constitutional government which, both before and since the Commonwealth, had placed every important office of the State in the hands of the nobility, clergy, and gentry, he had substituted his own righteous, personal rule reluctantly, and as the only possible means of upholding the glorious cause which had triumphed at the cost of so lavish an expenditure of blood. Now, for the first and only time in our history, England enjoyed the blessings of civil and religious liberty and equality; no invidious distinction of sect for political purposes now existed to desolate the land with its atrocities; the harmony and repose of the religious world was complete. At home the administration of the laws was prompt and impartial; reviving industry and extending commerce scattered plenty; abroad England had reached her highest pinnacle of glory. Our invincible fleets—reappearing in the Mediterranean for the first time since the Third Crusade—coerced or crushed the piratical states of Barbary. Italy submitted to our just demands; but Holland and Spain, braving the Protector's wrath, were in succession smitten, bleeding to his feet, never to recover from their panic-fear during the lifetime of their conqueror. The Puritan hero had made good his proud but patriotic boast, "that he would render the name of an Englishman as much feared and revered as ever was that of a Roman." But in annihilating the kingly, aristocratic, and spiritual power, and in effacing the privileged classes, he had evoked a host of traditional and implacable enemies and slanderers, whose existence will be coeval with that of the interests they represent.

On the 30th of January, 1661, the demons of royal and aristocratic revenge and hate tore the rotting carcass of the immortal Oliver from its grave, and dragged it to Tyburn on a hurdle. There they went through the ghastly farce of hanging and mutilating, as an attainted traitor, our dead patriot and hero, who alive had made the stoutest of them quake and tremble. His body they flung into a hole at the gallows' foot, but that glorious head of his, whose nod so lately shook the world, they stuck upon a pole to scare and terrify the people whom he had freed and loved so well. Thus did our Norman Caste repay the magnanimous victor of Newbury, Marston Moor, and Naseby, of Preston, Dunbar, and Worcester, for their lives, honours, and estates, which his conquering arm had won from them, but which his clement heart gave back.

IV.

RESTORATION OF THE NORMAN MONARCHY, ARISTOCRACY, AND CHURCH.

1660—1685.—The Commonwealth survived the great Protector for nearly two years, and was only subverted by the treachery and treason of Monk and Montague. These abandoned traitors having cashiered from the army and the fleet under their respective orders, the multitude of plebeian officers who at that glorious epoch had, for the first and only time in English history won distinction in their country's service, prepared to use the armed forces of the Republic thus emasculated, as their blind instruments for its destruction; and in

Restoration of the Norman Monarchy, &c. 125

exchange for a lavish bestowal of honours and wealth, to sacrifice, not simply the liberties of their country, but the lives of their companions in arms. And that famous renegade Lord Thomas Fairfax shares in this monstrous infamy and treason. Acting in concert with Monk in Scotland, he appears in arms at York, at the head of the nobility and gentry of the northern counties, and keeps open for the advance of his impenetrable ally, the high-road to London. Protesting to his Roundhead veterans, at each step, his boundless loyalty to the Commonwealth, which they were resolute to maintain, Monk marches rapidly southward, publicly canes an officer at York who charges him with the design of restoring Charles Stuart, and undisputed master of the metropolis, declares to General Ludlow, "Yea, we must live and die together for a Commonwealth" at the very moment when he had practically accomplished its complete annihilation. Then betrayed Puritanism fell on evil days and evil tongues, and persecution was again rampant in its midst.

A.D. 1660.—"Plain George Monk"—now become his Grace the Duke of Albemarle—had indeed restored the monarchy, but the legislative reconquest of England to the yoke of Anglicanism was effected and maintained by a vast and permanent conspiracy of the Court and caste, whose motives are best illustrated by the language of the chief actors themselves. Thoroughly cured of that love of liberty which, in setting them in battle-array against King Charles I., had immolated privilege with prerogative, the Roundheads of noble birth had deserted the popular cause, and rallied round the monarchy and Church, henceforth adopting Anglicanism as the sacred badge and symbol of their political unity and consequent supremacy. But the Puritan gentry, from whose ranks had sprung Cromwell and Hampden, Winthrop and Ireton, Pym and Endicott, the champions of popular liberty in both worlds, had given the death-blow to national sovereignty by their abandonment of the good old cause which was their glorious crown of immortality. "A common suffering," says Green, "had thrown the gentry and the episcopalian clergy together, and for the first time in our history the country squires were zealous for the Church." Indeed, it is scarcely an exaggeration to say that the political and social conditions and distinctions of the Norman Conquest were again revived in England. The King and the nobility, the landed gentry and the clergy, rescued by Monk—to their own amazement and in their own utter prostration—from political shipwreck, and restored without a blow to the vast heritage they had lost on the battle-field, confronted in a compact and hostile mass the democracy that had overwhelmed them. Their inglorious and bloodless triumph over the invincible but betrayed heroes of Marston Moor and Naseby, of Dunbar and Worcester, had inflamed rather than allayed their hatred of their late plebeian conquerors, to whose magnanimity under the Commonwealth they were alone indebted for the preservation of their lives, honours, and estates; and burning with shame and indignation at the subversion of their supremacy, which, founded in brute force and universal confiscation, had been transmitted from father to son in an unbroken line of succession extending over a period of six hundred years, and intent on repairing the ravages of the late Revolution and preventing its recurrence, they resolved to reduce England to the ancient servitude by means of atrocious legislation that should be as effectual of its purpose as their ancestors' swords which achieved the original Conquest, whilst possessing the additional virtue of enabling them thenceforward to appeal to the sanctity and majesty of the law in justification of their usurpation and tyranny; and having packed, by the corruptest practices, the infamous Cavalier or Pension Parliament, which was composed for the most part of young men, who were, says Pepys, "the most profane swearing fellows that ever I heard in my life," that odious legislature—the first-fruits of the complete reconciliation of Court and caste—proceeded in cold blood with its horrid work of reconstruction and revenge.

"We have thought," said King Charles in his Declaration to the House of Lords from Breda, "we have thought it very fit and safe for us to call to you for your help in composing the distempers and distractions of the kingdom, in which your sufferings are next to those we have undergone ourselves, and therefore you cannot but be the most proper counsellors for removing these mischiefs and preventing the like for the future." And now, addressing the Cavalier Parliament—which he had literally commissioned after "so many and great revolutions to provide proper remedies for those evils" and "to raise up the banks and fences which have been cast down"—the King declared: "We can never differ but in judgment, and that must be when I do not rightly express myself or you do not rightly understand me; but our interest is so far linked together that we can never disagree." "In God's name," said the King, "in God's name provide full remedies for any future mischiefs. Be as severe as you will against any new offenders, especially if they be so upon the old principles, and pull up those principles by the roots." But he deprecates any infringement of the Act of Indemnity as endangering "the good disposition and security we are all in," and also as the "breach of a promise I so solemnly made when I was abroad," and concluded his speech by referring "the rest to the Chancellor." And accordingly the Lord Chancellor Clarendon told them: "You ought to thank God that after all the prodigies in Church and State you have lived to see the King at the opening of Parliament." . . . "You are the great physicians of the kingdom, and, God knows, have many wayward and froward and distempered patients."

And singling out the Puritan clergy as especial objects of vengeance, he proceeded: "There is a sort of your patients which I must recommend to your utmost vigilance, utmost severity, and in no part to your lenity or indulgence; such who are so far from valuing your prescriptions, that they look not upon you as their physicians but their patients. . . . These are the seditious preachers . . . who, by repeating the very expressions and teaching the very doctrine they set on foot in the year 1640, sufficiently declare that they have no mind that twenty years should put an end to the miseries we have undergone." Their "preaching has," says he, "all the marks by which good men are taught to know and avoid the sin against the Holy Ghost." And he declares: "If you do not provide for the thorough quenching of these firebrands, king, lords, and commons shall be their meanest subjects, and the whole kingdom kindled into one general flame." He next referred, in the strangest language, to the attempted riot in the streets of London, of about fifty or sixty millenarians, the main body of whom, headed by their leader—a cooper of the name of Venner—Colonel Corbet, with nine horsemen only, had charged and utterly routed in Wood Street. "The most desperate," says he, "and prodigious rebellion broke out in this city that hath been heard of in any age; and by the multitude of intercepted letters from and to all the counties of England, in which the time was set down wherein the 'Work of the Lord' was to be done, by the desperate carriage of the traitors themselves and the bragging of their friends, it may be concluded the combination reached very far; and if the indefatigable industry of the Lord Mayor had not prevented it, probably the fury would not have been extinguished before this famous city, or a great part of it, had been burnt to ashes; therefore it will become your wisdoms to provide new remedies for new diseases, and to secure the precious person of our dear Sovereign from the first approaches of villainy, and the peace of the kingdom from the first overtures of sedition." And this attempted riot, with the suppositious plot which he at once concocted and denounced, served as pretexts for the initiation—under the mask of religion—of the most cold-blooded, prolonged, and deadly political persecution recorded in our history.

With a vivid recollection of that disunion in

spiritual matters which had led to their political effacement under the Commonwealth, the King and his advisers resolved to reconstruct the old monarchical and aristocratic constitution upon those ancient ecclesiastical foundations which had been its firm support through so many ages, and the undermining of which had alone laid the glittering superstructure in the dust. "How much," says the King, "how much the peace of the State is concerned in the peace of the Church, and how difficult a thing it is to preserve order and government in civil, whilst there is no order or government in ecclesiastical affairs, is evident to the world; and this little part of the world, our own dominions, hath had so late experience of it that we may very well acquiesce in the conclusion without enlarging ourself in discourse upon it, it being a subject we have had frequent occasion to contemplate upon, and to lament abroad as well as at home." And after professing his own high affection and esteem for the Church, "the reverence to which hath supported us, by God's blessing, against many temptations," he expresses the hope that all men will acknowledge "the support of the episcopal authority to be the best support of religion, by being the best means to contain the minds of men within the rules of government." And the Lord Chancellor, Clarendon, the King's chief adviser and absolute guide in ecclesiastical matters, bluntly declared that all the enemies of the Church, without distinction of individual or sect, were also the enemies of the existing political system. And in pursuance of these views the Anglican Church was re-established; those of the ejected bishops who were still alive were restored to their sees; the vacancies in the episcopal bench were filled up; the surviving episcopalian clergy returned to their benefices; the Liturgy was again read in the churches; and, finally, in order to secure the rising generation, to the Church alone was entrusted the direction of the education as well as the religion of the nation. And the Church was not slow in demonstrating its zeal and fervour for the interests of the monarchy and aristocracy who had revived it, and to whom it was a political necessity. That monarchy, whose restoration had hung on so slender a thread, that Monk had declared, after he had cashiered his Republican officers, "the army are jealous of me that a king is at the bottom of this design," and had warned Charles, through Sir Charles Grenville, even after his occupation of London, that "while no one wished his Majesty greater felicity, or with greater passion desired his restoration, yet if it were not cautiously attempted it would be out of his power to serve him in it"—that monarchy, in a word, which Monk—whose cool and steadfast mendacity staggered and confounded friends and foes alike—had founded in treason, fraud, and intrigue, was now declared by the Church to be a divine institution, and passive obedience and non-resistance articles of religion; whilst her own politico-ecclesiastical organization, which had perished twenty years before in the blood and crimes of Laud, but which the Popish Charles had resuscitated, for avowedly political purposes, was again loudly and unblushingly proclaimed the only true and Apostolic Church. Henceforth, Anglicanism is to knit into a holy and indissoluble brotherhood the monarchy and the privileged classes. Under the banner of the Church, the new crusaders march from victory to victory, till every citadel of power is stormed. Masters of Parliament, of place, of public instruction, the nobility, clergy, and gentry might make a prouder and truer boast than the Grand Monarque himself, and say, "We are both Church and State." Indeed, they mould the mind of England at their will, or crush resistance, and, in the name of monarchy itself, eclipse the splendours of the Crown.

We must now relate the notorious, yet necessary, details of this legislative reconquest of England. The Cavalier Parliament ordered that upon a certain day all of its members should publicly receive the Communion according to the Anglican ritual, on pain of expulsion, and that the various Acts of the Long Parliament, which had abolished the monarchy, Church, and House of Lords, should be burnt by the common hangman. The last strongholds of the Republicans, the boroughs, were wrested from them by the Corporation Act, which excluded all but Anglicans, not simply from the municipalities, but from the magistracy, and from all civil offices in every county and town. This measure gave to the nobility and landed gentry—who, as possessors of the soil, were already masters of the counties—a controlling influence over the parliamentary representation of the boroughs, as electoral rights were either exclusively restricted to members of the corporations, or limited to so small a portion of the inhabitants as to render the governing bodies always paramount; and, from time immemorial, those municipal cliques had practically surrendered the electoral franchise they dared not freely exercise to the neighbouring aristocracy or the Crown. By the renewal of the Act of Uniformity, or rather by the passage of a new Act, whose more stringent conditions of conformity were framed expressly for the expulsion of the Puritan clergy, attendance at the parish church on Sundays and holidays was made universally compulsory, under the severest penalties. This odious Act further exacted from all private and public schoolmasters, and tutors, not in holy orders—who were to receive episcopal license on pain of three months' imprisonment—as well as from all clergymen—who must henceforth receive episcopal ordination—the oath of non-resistance, and a declaration, also on oath, of their approval of the entire contents of the newly-revised Liturgy; while all persons who dared to speak against the Book of Common Prayer —which had been a dead letter in England for twenty years—or to dispense with its use in their religious services, incurred the penalty of forfeiture of goods for the first offence, a year's imprisonment for the second, and imprisonment for life for the third. Moreover, all former laws and penalties for establishing religious uniformity were still to be in force, and applied to the present form. But political retaliation and revenge, under the garb of religious zeal, culminated in the Conventicle Act. This atrocious Act empowered any single magistrate to inflict on all persons above the age of sixteen who were at any meeting in a private house, where more than five persons were assembled besides the family, "under colour or pretence of any exercise of religion," which was not Anglican, a fine of five pounds or three months' imprisonment for the first offence, ten pounds or six months' imprisonment for the second, and for the third, on conviction by a jury, a hundred pounds or seven years' transportation to some American plantation—other than New England or Virginia, where they would have been received with open arms as blessed martyrs—and in the event of escape or return, the offenders were to suffer death, without benefit of clergy. For the better execution of this Act, in addition to the civil authorities, the militia and military were enjoined, on the certificate of any magistrate, to "dissolve or prevent any such unlawful meetings, and to take into custody all such persons as they shall think fit." Moreover, unlimited power was given to the miserable spies and informers who made a trade of infesting by day and night the homes of the Puritans. "This Act," so runs the preamble, "this Act, and all clauses of it, shall be construed most largely and beneficially for the suppressing of Conventicles, and for the justification and encouragement of all persons to be employed in the execution thereof." The Five Mile Act prohibited all Nonconforming ministers—unless they took the oath of non-resistance and swore never to attempt "any alteration of government in Church and State"—from approaching within five miles of any city, borough, or corporate town, or of any place where they had ever preached, under the penalty of a fine of fifty pounds and six months' imprisonment. Finally, on the pretence that the mere handful of English Roman Catholics endangered the stability of their despotism in Church and State, established by law, the Cavalier Parliament passed the Test Act, which excluded them from the public service, by exacting from all State officials the oath of allegiance and supremacy, together with a declaration against transubstantiation. Although ostensibly directed against the Roman Catholics alone, yet the Test Act, by an unscrupulous device, involving a parliamentary breach of faith, was made to include the Puritans, whom it doomed to political ostracism, by requiring all officeholders, civil or military, to be public communicants of the Anglican Church. This was the last of that black list of modern "bloody statutes"—the Corporation Act, the Act of Uniformity, the Conventicle, Five Mile, and Test Acts—which were expressly framed for the annihilation or conversion of the Puritan Republicans of England—we may say of the English nation itself, for it had been Puritanic for twenty years—and for the "pulling up by the roots" of those glorious principles of civil and religious liberty and national sovereignty which they had enthroned at home during the Commonwealth, and which their martyrs, the Pilgrim Fathers, planted for ever, when, landing on Plymouth Rock, they took possession of the New World. Thus did our caste and court reconquer England—this time by means of odious legislation—as completely and absolutely as their Norman ancestors had effected the first Conquest on the battle-field of Hastings. And armed with this terrible weapon they proceeded, with all due forms of law, to wreak on their late plebeian conquerors a cold-blooded, ferocious, and dastardly vengeance for their inglorious overthrows on so many famous battle-fields.

Anglicanism now emerged from its temporary eclipse more terrible than ever. For upwards of a century had its hierarchy diligently and unsparingly used the stake, the block, and the halter to enforce uniformity; but the prelates of the Restoration surpassed all their predecessors in the enormity and magnitude of their atrocities. The scaffolds streamed with the best blood of Puritanism. The prisons, vile and pestilential dens which baffle description, were crowded to suffocation with the martyrs. "I saw," writes the Anglican Pepys, "I saw several poor creatures carried by, by constables for being at a conventicle. They go like lambs, without any resistance. I would to God they would either conform, or be more wise and not be catched." "Dr. Manton," writes another contemporary, "though he had great friends and mighty promises of favour, was sent prisoner to the Gatehouse for preaching the

Gospel in his own house in the parish where he had been formerly minister, and for not taking the Oxford oath and yet coming within five miles of a Corporation; and he continued there six months, and all that time (1670) the meetings in London were disturbed by bands of soldiers, to the terror of many and the death of some." " Above four hundred," says Crosby, " were crowded into Newgate, besides many more in the other prisons belonging to the city and parts adjacent." Twelve thousand Quakers alone were incarcerated at one time, of whom three hundred and sixty-nine were released from their sufferings by death. The total number of those who perished—amongst whom were Joseph Alleyne and Vavasour Powell—in those horrid dungeons in the reign of Charles II. was nearly eight thousand, and of the countless host who suffered for conscience' sake the names of sixty thousand have been left on record. In their insatiable thirst for revenge on their conquerors, whom disunion alone had vanquished without a struggle, the sanctity of death was not respected by the enemies of the Puritans. The graves were ransacked, and made to yield up to the cord, knife, and axe of the executioner, the sacred relics of the heroes of the Commonwealth. With the ferocity and barbarism of cannibals the Anglicans—who, like the Nihilists, had preached and practised political assassination; had foully murdered both Dorislaus and Ascham, our republican ambassadors at the Hague and Madrid, and had repeatedly attempted to assassinate great Oliver himself—mutilated the putrid bodies of men whom in life they had never encountered on the field of battle but to be utterly routed. They descended even to a lower depth of infamy, which was the lowest. The Church, in its zeal for the cause of its restorer and patron, one of the most immoral of monarchs, affected to regard as a desecration of Westminster Abbey the sepulchres of the saint-like mother of the Protector and of his favourite daughter. And the sacrilegious hands of its myrmidons, to whom nothing was sacred, plucked from their graves the bodies of those noble women, and thrust them—together with the remains of all the illustrious dead that had been interred in the Abbey during the Commonwealth—into a common and obscure trench.

The Puritan ministers were deprived of their livings *en masse* for refusing to conform, and were replaced by Anglican clergymen, notorious for their "pride and debauchery." And this expulsion on St. Bartholomew's day of two thousand Cromwellian rectors and vicars from their parishes and homes, to face henceforward their everlasting foes, poverty and persecution, completed the triumph of Anglicanism, and ushered in the reign of all the vices. National honour revelled in this universal saturnalia. The victorious fleet of Holland, sweeping the seas, ascends our rivers, devastating everything in its course. The Metropolis, wasted by plague and fire, was at its mercy, and was only saved from utter ruin by the invaders' ignorance of its defenceless condition. So low had England fallen that it was reported the Grand Monarque, the servile ally of Cromwell, had said in jest, "He knows no reason why his cousin the King of England should not be as willing to let him have his kingdom as that the Dutch should take it from him." The betrayed and deluded nation was now restored to its right mind. "It is strange," writes Pepys, "it is strange how everybody do nowadays reflect upon Oliver and commend him, what brave things he did, and made all the neighbour princes fear him."

But scarcely had England, stripped of her ancient military renown, been again laid prostrate at the feet of her old masters than their unholy alliance was snapped asunder. Court and caste alike claim supremacy, and the despised and ignorant multitude, deprived of every vestige of political power, is in turn the dupe and victim of either cynical combatant. Yet King Charles was the reluctant and involuntary accomplice of the aristocracy and Church in their ferocious and wanton persecution of his Dissenting subjects. Satisfied with the political annihilation of the Republicans, with the execution as traitors of a moiety of his father's judges, and with the judicial murder of Sir Harry Vane, which he deemed a dire necessity of politics, the King compelled the House of Lords—who would have excepted from a general pardon every servant of the late Republic—to pass a Bill of Indemnity, declaring that he would ever hold good the sacred promise he had made at Breda, without which neither he nor they would have been restored to their lost rights. And infamous as was the private character of the King, it is impossible to doubt the sincerity of his endeavours to secure liberty of conscience to all his subjects, seeing that the whole course of his reign—which might have been one of profound personal tranquillity and satisfaction had he silently assented to persecution—was a long and unsuccessful struggle with the aristocracy and Church for the attainment of that object. "I shall never think him a wise man," said Charles to the Cavalier Parliament, "or that he can be my friend or wish me well, who would persuade me ever to consent to the breach, in the least degree, of a promise I so solemnly made when I was abroad and performed with that solemnity." And prompted by sentiments of honour and humanity, and perhaps by the personal conviction of the inherent right of all people to freedom of conscience, the King attempted to mitigate the ferocity of legislation, which he was powerless to control, by granting a royal dispensation from its penalties. And on the 26th of December, 1662, in moderate and guarded terms, in order to avoid offence or surprise, he issued his first Declaration of Indulgence. After expressing his firm adhesion to the Act of Uniformity and his abhorrence of military and arbitrary power, he referred to his promise of liberty of conscience contained in his Declaration of Breda, and said: "That as in the first place he had been zealous to settle the uniformity of the Church of England in discipline, ceremony, and government, and shall ever constantly maintain it; so, as for what concerns the penalties upon those who, living peaceably, do not conform themselves thereunto, through scruple and tenderness of misguided conscience, but modestly and without scandal perform their devotions in their own way, he would make it his special care, so far as in him lay, without invading the freedom of Parliament, to incline their wisdom next approaching sessions to concur with him in making some such Act for that purpose as may enable him to exercise with a more universal satisfaction that power of dispensing, which he conceived to be inherent in him." And in his speech on the reassembling of Parliament he gently referred to the declaration he had issued, and in the hope of procuring for it a Parliamentary sanction, mildly observed "that if the Dissenters would demean themselves peaceably and modestly he could heartily wish he had such a power of Indulgence to use upon occasion."

But the Cavalier Parliament—who brought to their task of reconstructing the British Constitution a collective conscience and responsibility which could afford to set at defiance every principle of right and justice, of patriotism and pity—would tolerate no check on their absolute power. In their judgment, the Restoration system could only permanently be maintained by the conversion of the English nation to Anglicanism, which they thought might easily be effected by a constant, indiscriminate, and rigorous enforcement of the "solid and lasting" laws provided for that purpose. And a committee of the House represented to the King in hollow, yet significant terms, that they had considered the nature of the Declaration of Breda, and were humbly of opinion that they could absolve him from it. That the Indulgence professed would establish schism by law, increase sects and sectaries, undermine the authority, and endanger the existence of the Church, and tend to dissolve the very bonds of government. That it would give Dissenters an "opportunity to count their numbers," and "lead directly and inevitably to open disturbance." But, on the contrary, "that the asserting of the laws and the religion established, according to the Act of Uniformity, is the most probable means to produce a settled peace and obedience throughout your kingdom." And, in conclusion, they assure the King, while forcing him to withdraw his Declaration of Indulgence, and to assent to a fiercer persecution of his Dissenting subjects, that "if any persons shall presume to disturb the peace of the kingdom, we do in all humility declare that we will for ever, and in all occasions, be ready with our utmost endeavour and assistance to adhere to and serve your majesty, according to our bounden duty and allegiance."

Meanwhile, King Charles — the rightful heir of the Norman Conqueror, who had founded the Anglican Church, and bestowed on the ancestors of our aristocracy their honours and estates, nay, who had forced them against their will to conquer England — would not consent to meekly play the part of a mere king in name; but persisted in his endeavours to achieve, not for a moment the political enfranchisement of his people, whom he ever regarded with "great clemency and tenderness," but their deliverance from wanton persecution. It is true that the only matter wherein the King and Parliament could seem to differ was that of Indulgence and Toleration—for so the canting and insulting phrase ran—to Nonconformists, which Charles, solemnly pledged by his Declaration of Breda, and by his personal promises to the Presbyterian clergy, had always betrayed a great desire to grant; but the breach could not fail to widen. And when a deputation of Dissenting ministers, at the recommendation of Sir John Barber and others, waited on the King with an address, professing their loyalty and acknowledging his clemency, Charles told them: "Though such Acts have been made, I am against persecution, and hope ere long to stand on my own legs, and then you shall see how much I am against it." And the Dissenters, satisfied by the King's proposal of Indulgence, that he had the will if not the power to deliver them at least from persecution, were encouraged to resist comprehension in a Church which was to them the badge of temporal, as well as spiritual servitude, flattering themselves with the constant hope of royal toleration.

But the Lords and Commons, the bishops and clergy, believing that a relaxation of their sanguinary laws, enforcing conformity to Anglicanism and imposing Anglican tests, would shatter at a blow their carefully-reconstructed constitution in Church and State, now proceeded to defend that *régime* of tyranny and persecution by the novel pretence that nothing could more encourage and promote Popery than an Indulgence of Protestant Dissenters, while nothing could so effectually secure the peace of the kingdom as the suppression of both. They then proceeded to sow divisions between the King and people, whom they had outwitted and overpowered, and whose coalition they feared, by attacking the Court on its weak side, its inclination to Roman Catholicism, and by raising the sinister and ominous cry of " No Popery." So long as the King, from fear of the Revolution, had headed the nobility, clergy, and gentry in their legislative reconquest of England, the Cavalier Parliament had advocated the widest stretch of the royal prerogative; but no sooner does that genial and clement voluptuary, touched with pity, recoil from the wanton persecution of his people, who had acclaimed his return, than those " profane swearing " legislators, ensconced within their impregnable Parliamentary fortress, pose as the champions of the majesty and sanctity of the law and of the " true Protestant religion " enthroned in Anglicanism; and with unexampled and unabashed effrontery those wily phrasemongers denounce the King's dispensing and suspending power as subversive of the Constitution in Church and State, and his toleration of Dissenters as a cloak for the encouragement of Papists; and with ghastly irony, yet marvellous finesse, they brand their unhappy Puritan victims, who simply desired immunity from persecution, as the instruments of arbitrary power and the tools and engines of the Church of Rome. Nay, more, resorting to their favourite and habitual weapons of calumny, mendacity, and cant, the Malignants, in order to divert public attention from their own real and abiding tyranny, indirectly attacked the Court by inflaming the bigotry and rancour of the illiterate and credulous multitude against the mere handful of their Roman Catholic fellow-countrymen, whom they accuse of entertaining the preposterous design of proselytizing Protestant England, of subverting the existing Government, and of establishing Popery and arbitrary power amidst universal massacre and conflagration, at the same time protesting that the free and indiscriminate enforcement of their bloody statutes—the only effectual bulwark, say they, now against Popery—could alone save the nation from such unspeakable horrors. And the immoral device had its desired effect, for the Dissenters — indeed, we may say the nation, which had been Puritanic — stripped of all political and social influence by the secession from their ranks of the Puritan nobility and landed gentry, deprived of all intellectual training save that imparted by Anglican priests and schoolmasters, and decimated by relentless and cruel persecution, while too weak to defend their own project of liberty, were yet averse to a toleration that would have embraced the Papists, many of them declaring that they would "suffer anything" rather than appear to promote Popery. And the King, abandoned by "God's silly people," as he somewhat irreverently called the Dissenters, and confronted by the combined privileged classes, ready to do battle for the terrible legislation which had practically enthroned them, was constrained to confound in a common persecution both Puritans and Papists, and to link, brand, and suppress them as the common enemies of Church and State.

They extorted from the King a proclamation for the banishment, by a given day, of all Popish priests and for the enforcement of the penal laws against all Popish recusants and such as were suspected of being so; and although Charles, in his speech of the 10th of February, 1667, had strongly recommended to both Houses "That you would seriously think of some course to beget a better union and composure in the minds of my Protestant subjects in matters of religion, whereby they may be induced not only to submit quietly to the Government, but also cheerfully give their assistance to the support of it," yet in their reply the Cavalier Parliament, contemptuously ignoring the royal motion, humbly petitioned his Majesty "That he would issue out his proclamation for enforcing the laws against Conventicles, and that care might be taken for the preservation of the peace of the kingdom against unlawful assemblies of Papists and Nonconformists." And accordingly the King, destitute alike of principle and power, was induced to publish the required proclamation, in expectation of a liberal subsidy from the Commons. Again and again they extorted from the reluctant but dependent monarch like acts of submission, and as often both Houses of the Cavalier Parliament "returned to his Majesty their thanks for his care of the public in issuing out his proclamation for suppressing Conventicles, and humbly desired his Majesty to continue the same care for the future."

But the struggle between the Court and caste was only temporarily suspended, and on its resumption it assumed wider and more sinister proportions. The Anglicans, who had made war on Holland in 1664, to prevent it from giving shelter and assistance to their Republican fellow-countrymen, no sooner found their own tyranny menaced by the King than they formed a close and traitorous connection with John de Witt, the Pensionary, whilst Charles, with a sagacity which subsequent events sadly demonstrated, entered into an alliance with France for the partition—reserving, however, sovereign rights for his nephew over certain provinces—of Holland, the centre of intrigue against his Government, the powerful auxiliary of his disaffected nobility, clergy, and gentry, and the formidable rival of his realm.

At this juncture the Prince of Orange, at the instigation of his mother, the King's sister, resolved to visit England, ostensibly to solicit his uncle's interest and support in his ambitious designs on Holland and to demand payment of certain sums claimed by the Princess Dowager; but no doubt his polestar was the English crown, where his ambition was so soon to centre and so near to which he stood by right of birth. By a secret article of the Treaty of Westminster (April 5, 1654) the Dutch, in abject submission to the inexorable will of Oliver Cromwell, their conqueror, had pledged themselves under the great seal of the States never to admit the Prince of Orange or any descendant of King Charles I. to be their stadtholder, general, or admiral, and the Perpetual Edict had solemnly ratified this exclusion. But the disinherited Prince, who had been lately chosen First Noble of Zealand, and had now reached his twentieth year, began, in the quaint but suggestive language of Sir William Temple, our ambassador at the Hague, "to shew himself very forward, and to deserve the Character of being a most extreme, hopeful Prince: And to speak more plainly, something much better than he expected, a young Man of more Parts than ordinary, and of the better sort, that is, not lying in that Kind of Wit which was neither of Use to one's self nor any body else, but in good plain Sense, which shews Application, if he had Business that deserved it, and with extreme good and agreeable Humour and Dispositions, and thus far of his way without any Vice: besides being sleepy always by ten a Clock at Night, and loving Hunting as much as he hated Swearing, and preferring Cock-Ale before any Wine."

Before setting out the Prince of Orange, with his habitual caution, earnestly pressed his admiring gossip, but unconscious tool, Sir William Temple, for his opinion as to his chances of success in England, saying that "all his best friends in Holland were of opinion, that in case that should wholly fail him, his journey would prove of great prejudice to his affairs at home, by letting his friends see how little he was considered by his Majesty, whose countenance would be a great support to him in the course of his fortunes." The King, who seemed already instinctively to distrust his treacherous kinsman, discouraged and deferred from time to time his journey; but Dutch William, like his Norman namesake—to contrast a pigmy with a giant—was not to be diverted from any fixed design. He embarked at Brill, October 27th, 1670, upon one of his Majesty's yachts that waited there for him, and arrived at Margate on October 29th, and since the Conqueror appeared at the Confessor's Court, no foreigner has landed on our shores so wantonly destructive of the English race as he. The Court received him with royal honours, and the caste with enthusiasm, as if they already recognized in him their natural leader and protector in their struggle with the King for the maintenance of their absolute supremacy in Church and State. The Lord Mayor, Aldermen and Sheriffs of London wait upon him with a congratulatory address, and subsequently entertain him with extraordinary magnificence at Drapers' Hall. He is received with every mark of distinction by both universities; Oxford conferring on him and on distinguished members of his suite honorary degrees. For nearly four months he protracted his portentous visit, which was ominously associated with Rochester, where he passed his first night on English soil, and whence he took his final departure (February 15th, 1671). And although he had obtained no satisfaction of his claims, yet he expressed himself "infinitely sensible of the great tenderness and affection expressed to him by their Majesties during the time he had been in England, and not less satisfied with the universal esteem and respect of the Court and people here." And in all human probability the Prince of Orange at this time initiated his dark conspiracy with the privileged classes for the mutual maintenance of their respective interests and pretensions.

A.D. 1672-1674.—Before entering on his second Dutch War, the King issues his second Declaration of Indulgence, wherein he asserts that his care for the preservation of the rights and interests of the Church had been sufficiently manifested by the whole course of his government, and by the many and frequent ways of coercion that had been used for reducing the nation to religious uniformity. "But," continues he, "it being evident by the sad experience of twelve years, that there is very little fruit of all these forcible courses, we think ourselves obliged to make use of that supreme power in ecclesiastical matters which is not only inherent in us, but hath been declared and recognized to be so by several statutes and Acts of Parliament." Therefore, in order to quiet the minds of his subjects in matters of religion, to induce foreigners to settle in their midst, to encourage trade and commerce, and to prevent dangers that might arise from private meetings and seditious Conventicles, he suspended all penal laws against Nonconformists and Papists, and set free the hosts of martyrs who thronged his gaols, whose numbers are not recorded, but may be fairly guessed from the fact that twelve thousand members of the petty sect of Quakers alone were released by this very act. The Nonconformists were allowed by special license to erect for their own use, in all parts of the kingdom, a sufficient number of public places of worship, but the Papists were restricted in the exercise of their religion to their own houses. Yet the King deems it prudent, from fear of the aristocracy and Church, to warn all his subjects that should they presume to abuse this liberty and preach seditiously, or "to the derogation of the doctrine, discipline, or government of the Established Church," he should proceed against them with the utmost rigour, testifying at once his severity ·to punish offenders, and his indulgence "to truly tender consciences."

But the nobility, clergy, and gentry, who lived in constant dread of the recurrence of their dismal fate under the Commonwealth, and who believed the atrocious penal laws to be an indispensable bulwark against the democracy, were prepared to sacrifice both dynasty and nation in their defence. Therefore the " profane swearing members " of the Cavalier Parliament humbly represent to the King that, considering the Declaration of Indulgence, they found themselves bound in duty to inform him that Penal Statutes, in matters ecclesiastical, cannot be suspended but by Act of Parliament; in other words, by themselves, who had specially passed those Acts—in terror of the Republic, which had been their grave—as legal guarantees for the security and perpetuity of their strangely recovered ascendency. The King—most probably influenced by his mother's early teaching, as well as disgusted and repelled by the ferocity and canting hypocrisy of resuscitated Anglicanism—was at heart a Romanist, and the Duke of York an avowed adherent of Rome, and on this peg the aristocracy and Church now hung the defence of their monstrous despotism. King Charles's Declaration of Indulgence, which sprang undoubtedly from "his great clemency and tenderness to his people," they call a violation of their glorious constitution in Church and State —for by that euphemism they henceforth designate the sovereign and despotic sway of the aristocracy and Church—an invasion of the legislative attributes of Parliament, and a mere cloak for the furtherance and final establishment of Popery and arbitrary power. And resorting to their old device of assailing Charles and James on their weak side, their secret or avowed conversion to the Catholic faith, they proceed to rouse and inflame—by declamation in the churches as elsewhere—the passions and bigotry of the ignorant and deluded multitude against their Catholic fellow-countrymen and the Court, by raising the specious yet false cry of apprehension and alarm at the growth of Popery and arbitrary power. And a few days afterwards they presented to His Majesty another address, humbly representing that the best means, in their opinion—parodying his own words—"for the satisfying and composing the minds of his subjects," would be a free and indiscriminate persecution of both Puritans and Papists, by the rigorous enforcement of the odious Penal Laws, which had been avowedly enacted for the annihilation of the Republicans and their principles, but which they now pretended were the most effectual defence against the ghastly spectre Popery, they conjured up at will, to scare the nation and confuse opinion as to the true character of their conflict with the Court. Finally, the Cavalier Parliament—whose grants of money to the King had always been limited and periodical, so that, as they said, he might the oftener have need of them —absolutely refused to grant supplies until the Declaration of Indulgence was withdrawn. And the King was again obliged to abandon his people—destitute alike of leaders and organization, and the unconscious dupes of the real and enduring conspiracy of the aristocracy and Church—to the fierce tempest of persecution, which was the bitter penalty they had to pay for their unpardonable crime of routing on so many glorious battlefields the proud descendants of our Norman Conquerors, and freeing England, for a brief space, from their cruel yoke.

Meanwhile, events on the Continent had given the Dutch ally of the aristocracy and Church an opportunity of displaying his courage, exercising his matchless skill in intrigue, and gratifying his ambition in his native land. Placing themselves under his leadership and protection, they had necessarily adopted his Dutch foreign policy as their own most insane English policy, and were paving the way, more or less unconsciously, for the transference of the destinies of their country into the hands of a profound but unprincipled politician, who would recklessly squander the blood and treasure of England in furtherance of his own ambitious and impracticable military projects. This Dutch prince of German lineage, frail and emaciated in body, but astute and vigorous in mind, was a striking example of strength and capacity in the midst of dangers. At the age of twenty-two he had been appointed, in violation of the Perpetual Edict, and in the teeth of John de Witt's most strenuous opposition, commander of his country's armies. It was an hour of greatest danger. Louis XIV. and Charles II. had commenced their unprovoked war with the avowed object of subjugating Holland. The French armies, commanded by the great Marshals Turenne and Condé, had occupied the country almost without opposition as far as Amsterdam. This moment of national calamity had been seized by the aristocratic adherents of the Prince as a golden opportunity for destroying their ruling democratic rivals. An obscure miscreant, of the name of Teikel, had revealed a pretended plot of Cornelius de

Witt, the brother of the Grand Pensionary, to assassinate the Prince of Orange. The deluded rabble, believing themselves betrayed, had risen in revolt, and, headed by Orange chiefs—who, at the instigation of the Prince, subsequently rewarded the murderers—had torn in pieces the Grand Pensionary, John de Witt, and his brother in the streets of the capital, and had overthrown the democratic constitution of Holland. The popular cry is for William, who, undismayed in this terrible crisis, assumes the management of affairs. His military operations are, as usual, unsuccessful; there is a clamour for peace. Knowing that the fate of Holland is in his hands, the combined monarchs, Louis and Charles, tempt the astute Prince to abandon a glorious struggle which promised to his lofty ambition so rich a harvest of political and military renown, with the bribe of the sovereignty of the meagre wrecks of that shattered State; but in vain. When Buckingham, Charles's envoy—with whom he temporized, and whom he tricked—losing all patience, haughtily asked him whether he did not himself perceive that Holland was lost, the wily Dutchman—assured of speedy succour from Germany and Spain—coolly replied, "There is one certain way by which I can be sure never to see it lost, I will die in the last ditch." His counter-declaration to one of his greatest confidants, whilst utterly destructive of this measured bombast, which was his ordinary vehicle of dissimulation, still indicates his fixed determination to prosecute the war at all hazards, short of the supreme one of self-immolation. "I am resolved," said he, on being asked how he intended to live when Holland was lost, "I am resolved to live upon my lands in Germany, and I would rather spend my life in hunting there than sell my country and liberty to France at any price." His spirit reanimates others, the dykes are cut, the country is inundated, and the hosts of France are compelled to retire. There is a reaction, an uprising in Europe in their favour. The Cavalier Parliament compels Charles to conclude a separate treaty with Holland; Spain and the Empire coalesce against France, and Holland is saved. But saved at the expense of the loyalty and patriotism of the English aristocracy. "I will confess to you," said the Prince of Orange, in a confidential conversation with Sir William Temple, our ambassador at the Hague, "I will confess to you that during the late war, neither the States, nor myself in particular, were without application made to us from several persons, and considerable ones too in England, who would fain have engaged us to head the discontents that were raised by the conduct of the Court in that whole war, which I knew was begun and carried on quite contrary to the humour of the nation "—ignorant he should have added of his enduring plot with the privileged classes against themselves, whose successful issue would lay two hundred thousand of their number into inglorious graves in Flanders— "and might," continued he, "and might perhaps have proved very dangerous to the crown, if it had not ended as it did." And although with his habitual astuteness he had declined to accede to their premature invitation to invade England, yet he had firmly established and consolidated his vast and permanent conspiracy with the aristocracy and Church, against the Stuart line and English nation, whose momentous consequences this ensuing history will unfold.

A.D. 1674-1678.—On the conclusion of peace with Holland, the King commanded Sir William Temple to represent to the

Prince of Orange that His Majesty knew of the treasonable practices of certain of his subjects, and would esteem it an infinite service if His Highness would reveal to him their names. But the Prince—who must have regarded with grim humour the innocent design of the King to draw from himself a disclosure of his own plot and partisans, blandly replied, "He was sure the King would not press him upon a thing so much against all honour, as to betray men who professed to be his friends." The alarmed monarch then despatches as his special envoy to the Hague the Earl of Arlington, who on his arrival told Sir William Temple: "That he was come over to set some things right between the King and Prince that he doubted were amiss, and to settle a perfect kindness and confidence between them for the future." But the Prince, who still maintained a close correspondence with the disaffected aristocracy and Church, and regulated his conduct by their advice, treated with scant courtesy the royal envoy. The King's overtures were curtly, or categorically, rejected, or set aside. He met the proposal of a secret treaty with King Charles to assist him against any rebels at home, by affecting to wonder: "That the King of England could be so ill-beloved, or so imprudent as to need such assistance." And upon mention being made of a match with the eldest daughter of the Duke of York, he curtly replied: "His fortunes were not in a condition for him to think of a wife." Moreover he expressed dissatisfaction with what he called the arrogance and insolence of Lord Arlington's expostulations, and declared that he spoke to him as if he were dealing with a child whom he might make to believe what he pleased, and behaved "as if"—and this reminds us of his descendant the immortal "Citron"—"he had taken himself for the Prince of Orange and him for Lord Arlington." In fine, this arch-conspirator, who in league with English traitors had already contemplated the dethronement of his uncle, declared that Arlington's language was so artificial and illusory that "everybody knew that he, who was a plain man, could not bear it," and added that if the King had "remembered he was his nephew, though nothing else," Lord Arlington would not have acted as he had done.

Soon after the failure of these negotiations, and just before the meeting of Parliament in

April, 1675, the King having heard that the Prince intended coming over to England against the approaching sessions, wrote to Sir William Temple, commanding him to hinder it, as if His Majesty believed some revolutionary design prompted such a visit. This the Prince denied, assuring Sir William Temple: "That Lord Arlington had indeed talked of a journey after the peace should be concluded, in the meantime he hoped the King would not suspect him guilty of any disrespectful thought; he was His Majesty's servant, and if he could do him no service he would at least do him no hurt. But if the King would be otherwise possessed he could not help it; he had desired the Ambassador to assure him that there had been no ground for such a report." And yet, notwithstanding this denial, the Prince received about the same time a letter from Lord Arlington, in which he reiterated his accusations; and of which in an excited manner His Highness complained to Sir William Temple, saying: "It was impertinent, and that he therein mentioned the foresaid imaginary resolution of his going over to England as a thing certain, and intended by him for raising heats in the Parliament and commotions in the kingdom, and added that it was like to prove but ill friendship between him and the King, if it was to be made with blows." And referring to a remark of the Earl's to the effect that the Dutch had some old wounds among them which would still bleed if care were not taken of them, the Prince said: "He knew well enough what was meant by that expression," for Arlington had told Monsieur Read, in England during the negotiations for the last peace, that the King could cause the Prince to be served as De Witt was, if he chose to set about it. Here he flew, or feigned to fly, into a violent passion against Lord Arlington, calling his "proceeding malicious and insolent," and said he would write to him what he deserved, but would never have any further communication with any of His Majesty's Ministers: he would write to the King himself.

The alarm of Charles at this dark and dangerous conspiracy of the Prince of Orange with the aristocracy and Church, found expression on the opening of Parliament in 1675. The Lord Keeper, addressing the Lords and Commons in the King's stead, after referring to the "calumnies and slanders" which had been levelled at the

Stuart dynasty from Holland, but which he trusted would only serve to give them fresh opportunities of testifying "their loyalty and zeal," concluded his speech with the following remarkable words: "You have all the reason in the world to make men see this; for you have the same monarchy to assert, the same Church to defend, the same interest of nobility and gentry to maintain, the same excellent King to contend for, and the same enemies to contend against." This appeal was not made entirely in vain. The hostility of the Cavalier Parliament to the Court had diminished since the peace. Destitute alike of principle and patriotism, it had complacently subsided into the common pensioner of Europe. Bribes from all sides were freely flowing into its capacious maw. It was notoriously in the pay of France, Spain, Germany, and Holland, who, in mutual emulation, distributed their money amongst its members. And the respective influence, in the Cavalier or Pension Parliament, of the chief contending powers of Europe, was in arithmetical proportion to their bribes.

Meanwhile, disasters in the field had modified the views and policy of the Prince of

Orange. He had been surprised and routed at Mount Cassel by his life-long rival in arms and constant conqueror, the celebrated Marshal Luxemburg. This was the first of that long series of reverses, extending without a break over two sanguinary wars—and culminating in our awful overthrow at Landen—whose ceaseless repetition drew from the Dutch "asthmatic skeleton" the petulant exclamation: "Can't I beat that little hump-back!" and from the invincible "upholsterer of Notre Dame" the contemptuous rejoinder: "How does he know I have got a hump-back? He has never seen it." Schooled by the catastrophe of Mount Cassel and its grave consequences, the Prince of Orange had reflected on his rash refusal to marry the eldest daughter of the Duke of York, and in the hope of repairing his broken fortunes by dragging England blindfold to his side, he now resolves on the matrimonial union he had before declined. But first, in his garden at Honslaerdyk, he secretly confers with his blind partisan, Sir William Temple, on this important project. And having made that perhaps unconscious traitor promise to answer him "as a friend, or, at least, an indifferent person, and not as the King's ambassador," he candidly confessed that, during the last Dutch war, a considerable section of the English aristocracy had repeatedly invited him to invade England with a foreign army, and, placing himself at their head, to overthrow the Stuart dynasty. He further declared it was at the instigation of "all these persons" that he had rejected, a brief year since, the proffered hand of the presumptive heiress to the English Throne. And fortified by the assurance of shallow Temple that the match "would be much for his interest and honour," he writes at once both to the King and Duke to solicit their favour in this matter and their leave to visit England. But William's overture was received with coldness, for Charles resented the refusal of his former offer, and was indignant at the Prince's intrigues with his subjects. Then the proud but subtle stadtholder, who, through his own folly, saw the Crown of England, with all its mighty possibilities slipping for ever from his grasp, humbles himself, and sends to England Mynheer Bentink—that "wooden man," as Marlborough called him, and the future founder of our ducal house of Portland—to beg the King's permission for the Prince's journey hither, in order that he might apologize to his uncles for his past offences, and set before them his future plans and policy. And when Lord Treasurer Danby—on whose advice and Temple's the Prince was acting at this juncture—hints that the proposed alliance might induce the Prince of Orange to abandon his English partisans and adopt the views and policy of the Court, King Charles consents to his coming over, on the condition that he returns before the opening of Parliament. But once allowed to land in England, the Prince, warmly supported by the Danby Ministry and by the disaffected privileged classes, could easily impose his will upon the Court. The King desired to adjust a plan of general pacification before the consummation of the marriage ; but the Prince declared that, as things then stood, his allies were likely to have hard terms of peace, and that, for his part, he never would sell his honour for a wife. That night, at supper, Temple called upon him, and found this perfect master of dissimulation in the worst apparent humour he had ever seen him. He declared that he regretted he had ever come to England, and resolved he would stay but two days longer, and then he would leave if the King persisted in his resolution of making the peace precede the marriage.

"But," said this petty foreign potentate, whom aristocratic treason had made master of the fate of England, and who resorted to the covert threat of civil war and Dutch invasion to coerce the King, "but," said he, "before I go the King must choose how we shall live together from henceforward; I am sure it must be as the greatest friends or as the greatest enemies." And, in obedience to the wishes of the Dutch stadtholder, Sir William Temple, early in the morning, repeated this tentative and inflated discourse to the King, and did not fail to represent and magnify the evil consequences of braving the Prince's threat of an open rupture, considering the disaffection of so many of his subjects, and the repeated invitations which several of the chiefest of them had sent both to the Prince and the States General during the whole course of the late war. The King listened attentively to the ultimatum of his nephew, and to its vigorous enforcement by Sir William Temple. Conscious of the isolation of his brother and himself, and intimidated by the wily and resolute bearing of the Prince and his English partisans, whose intrigues had already endangered his throne, the King reluctantly consented to the match. A.D. 1677. "Well," said he, in language which revealed his uncertain frame of mind, " well, I never was yet deceived in judging of a man's honesty by his looks, and, if I am not mistaken in the Prince's face, he is the honestest man in the world; and I will trust him, and he shall have his wife; and you shall go immediately and tell my brother so, and that it's a thing I am resolved on." The Duke received the royal message with surprise, but said: "The King shall be obeyed; and I should be glad if all his subjects learned of me to obey him. I tell him my opinion freely upon anything; but when that is done, and I know his pleasure upon it, I obey him." The Prince—the only actor in this mighty drama who measured its full import—was at first incredulous of the tidings; then, realizing the magnitude of his success, he fell upon the neck of Temple and embraced him, saying: "You have made me a very happy man, and that very unexpectedly."

We may here observe parenthetically that the Prince of Orange was at that time twenty-nine years of age, and the Princess Mary seventeen; that our Protestant hero enrolled among his mistresses Elizabeth Villiers, one of the maids of honour of his child-wife, whom he further outraged by a sullen and sulky demeanour until he had extorted from her her right of succession to the English throne.

A few days after the celebration of the marriage the King, the Duke, and Prince, assisted by the latter's partisans, Lord Danby and Sir William Temple, vainly conferred together upon a plan of pacification. The King's favour had facilitated the Prince's advancement to the stadtholderate; the King's hand, in giving him his bride, had placed the English crown within his reach; but the Prince, dead to every sentiment save that of personal ambition, now strives—in league with the disaffected aristocracy and Church, who sought to divert the public mind from home affairs by foreign broils—to force upon King Charles his miserable continental policy. The Dutch had warred successfully against the combined arms of France and England, and Holland had been saved. But saved too soon to satisfy the Prince of Orange, who, prompted by personal rancour and ambition, now poses as the champion and arbiter of Europe, and the rival and foil of the Grand Monarque, for whom and for the French he entertains an unconquerable hate, the outcome partly of King Louis's mordant scorn of his inflated " little cousin," and subsequently envenomed by a private feud, springing from the seizure of his petty principality of Orange. He had become, by the force of events, the central figure of a mighty coalition, and the commander of its armies; and, as his power expands, the lust of military glory, that eternal curse of princes, seizes him, and regulates his policy. Proud to be the accidental master of so many legions which peace would snatch from him, this offspring of the war dreads a general pacification as the grave of his military career, and the eclipse of his political consideration. When Temple told him Pensionary Fagel had said he thought the Dutch should make a separate peace, and that he did not know a man in Holland who was not of his mind, the Prince replied: "Yes, I am sure I know one, and that is myself, and I'll hinder it as long as I can; but if anything should happen to me, I know it would be done in two days." He wishes to prolong the war till he had accomplished the, for him, impossible task of reducing France to the limits fixed by the treaty of the Pyrenees; in other words till, sated with glory, he had beaten conquered and dismembered France to his feet. And now, forsooth, with Spain, the Empire, Europe at his back, he must constrain King Charles—and this was the immediate object of his marriage—to place the lives and fortunes of his people in the Prince's hand, to minister to his greatness. The King desired to effect an equitable peace, and pressed on all the belligerents the advisability of mutual concessions. He was even prepared to fight for the preservation of Flanders, for he had confessed "he could never live at ease with his subjects" if that country were held permanently by the French: short of that eventuality, however, and wisely, he was indisposed to involve England in continental complications. But the Cavalier Parliament—in secret league with the Prince of Orange, whose interests were both identical, and who had both, rising from their own ashes, destroyed the democratic constitutions of their respective countries, and had virtually enthroned in England and in Holland a vanquished aristocracy—but the Cavalier Parliament, I say, adopting the Dutch foreign policy of the future " great and glorious deliverer" of the aristocracy and Church, much to the indignation of the King, besought him to make no peace with France, till he had stripped her of all the territories which she had acquired since the Pyrenean treaty; and further passed a resolution praying him that "he would forthwith enter into an actual war with France." Moreover, they voted the King an address, in which "they besought him to conclude a league, offensive and defensive, with the States-General of the United Provinces, against the growth and power of the French King, and for the preservation of the Spanish Netherlands; and to contract such other alliances with the allies as should appear necessary for that purpose." This sinister proposition they supported with specious arguments, and—anticipating the language and the odious foreign policy of the Parliaments of our Dutch and German kings—they promised unlimited supplies for maintaining what they called the honour of the crown and the safety of the people. But King Charles, who had been always tender of the lives of his subjects, resolutely refused to second the ambitious and impracticable designs of the Prince of Orange, or to minister to the political requirements of the restored aristocracy and Church, to whose tranquil enjoyment of sovereign power, foreign warfare —under a King of English blood—was an absolute necessity. And Holland, perceiving that the time had not yet come for England, protected by her native king, to immolate herself to Dutch ambition and aggrandizement, concludes, unknown to the Prince, a separate and advantageous treaty with the French. But when he hears the peace of Nimeguen is signed—July 31, 1678—the Prince of Orange—who was by birth a cosmopolitan, whom no particular nationality could claim—maddened at seeing his mighty projects of ambition baffled, suddenly and treacherously attacks the army of the Duke of Luxemburg, resting securely on the faith of the treaty, and throws away in this disastrous fight some seven thousand lives, in the vain hope of forcing Holland to resume the war and England and King Charles to succour her. He fails, thanks to the patriotic constancy of the King, and the holocaust of victims he had slaughtered on the battlefield of St. Denis was but a barren sacrifice to his pure spite and passion.

The failure of the Prince and Parliament to fasten on King Charles their foreign policy—which ten years later cost us twenty years of sterile bloodshed, and inaugurated a century of wanton warfare with the French—precipitated their collision with the Court. Conscious that Charles and James—who with the vices common to their age and to the Prince of Orange, had yet as English princes a " great clemency and tenderness to their people "—would never willingly concur—although concurrence would have brought to both repose and safety and a ready acquiescence in any system of religion or foreign policy they might have chosen to adopt, even in that of assisting the French to ruin the Dutch—conscious, I say, that Charles and James would never willingly concur in the enforcement by atrocious and universal persecution of their odious Test and Penal Laws, which had at once enslaved the nation and eclipsed the power and splendour of the crown; nor adopt their nefarious and sanguinary foreign policy; the Cavalier Parliament resolved on the virtual subversion of the Stuart dynasty and the seizure and permanent retention of the Conqueror's throne. And taking advantage of the lucky accident of Charles and James's secret or avowed conversion to the Catholic faith, the Prince and Parliament accuse the Court—an accusation which the whole career of both the King and Duke belies, although they naturally and patriotically sought a French alliance as a counterpoise to the vast conspiracy against the nation and themselves, of the aristocracy and Church with the Dutch Prince and Ruling caste—of the preposterous design of Romanizing and enslaving England by means of the military power of France. And prompted by the maxim that "a bad title makes a good king," that is, a king subservient to the will of his makers, the privileged classes prepare to pave the way to the throne for the Prince of Orange, who as a foreigner—like their later German *protégés*—could never love or be beloved by Englishmen, and must, perforce, in order to retain his crown, indissolubly link the great name of King to the real and enduring conspiracy and usurpation of a caste. And on the pretence that a Catholic sovereign would endanger the constitution in Church and State, as they with grim and mocking humour style their despotism, the Cavalier Parliament resolve at once to force the King to disinherit his brother, and stultify himself by accepting a successor of their own selection, who is forthwith to be brought to England and formally recognized, in virtue of his wife, as the presumptive heir to the Stuarts' throne. To effect this monstrous revolution they resort to measures akin to those which led to the murder and mutilation of John and Cornelius de Witt by the deluded mob of the Hague, and to the consequent elevation to practically sovereign power of the Prince of Orange in Holland.

A.D. 1678-1682.—Within a fortnight of the signing of the peace of Nimeguen, the baffled conspirators suborn a gang of perjured miscreants to ruin the Duke of York, by denouncing his co-religionists, and subsequently the Duke himself, as the authors of that basest of all impostures and villainies, the horrid and detestable Popish Plot. The first and vilest of those sanguinary scoundrels, the foul and loathsome Titus Oates, finding that the King scouted and ridiculed his gross imposture, resolved to appeal to the mob—as the multitude were now for the first time contemptuously called — who, steeped in lamentable but involuntary ignorance, always listened with credulity to any defamation of the Catholics. For this purpose he made an affidavit of the truth of this pretended Plot of the Jesuits for the murder of the King and the subversion of the Protestant religion before Sir Edmundbury Godfrey—a magistrate of Westminster and a partisan of the Catholics —who, seeing on the list of the intended victims the name of one of his particular friends—the Secretary of the Duke of York—warned him of his danger. A few days afterwards the corpse of Godfrey was found in a ditch near London, with his own sword thrust through his heart with such force as to stick out at his back; but the absence of blood from the wound, a broad purple mark encircling his broken neck, and bruises on his breast, proved that he had been most foully murdered. But who were his murderers? The drops of wax which besmeared Sir Edmundbury's clothes were meant to indicate that he had been strangled at night by Jesuits, for in that age tapers were only used by Roman Catholic priests in their religious services, and by persons of the highest rank. But in all probability—as his death was necessary to the success of the Plot—the unhappy Godfrey was the forerunning victim of that long list of innocent men, whom Buckingham, Shaftesbury, and their accomplices—under the tutelage and in the interests of the Prince of Orange—had, with diabolical ingenuity and cruelty, doomed to the horrid death of traitors, in order, by sheer terror, to force the King, whom they made a participator in their atrocities, to consent to the exclusion of his brother from the throne. Yet these aristocratic terrorists and revolutionists, with their vile tools, declare that the murder was an attempt of the Jesuits to smother the Plot, and hang three servants of the Queen on the false charge of having strangled Godfrey in Her Majesty's palace, and in a certain chamber tenanted at that very moment by the King. Meanwhile they proceeded to utilize their monstrous crime. Anticipating the orgies of the *sans culottes* of France, they make a ghastly spectacle of Godfrey's corpse, parading it, with every mark of ostentation, through the principal streets of the metropolis, and afterwards exposing it in public for several days. But the crowning demonstration was the funeral. In front of the vast procession marched in full canonicals the Anglican clergymen of London; and behind the bier, a thousand gentlemen in mourning, including many members of the legislature, headed, and excited to outrage by their countenance and presence, their wretched dupes the mob—clamouring for the blood of the Catholics, a general massacre of whom seemed imminent. This was a repetition of the nefarious tactics of the Dutch aristocrats at the Hague, who, inflaming the rabble with the cry of a sham Plot to assassinate the Prince of Orange, had stifled the democratic republic of Holland in the blood of the De Witts. Happily the innate magnanimity of the English populace restrained their hands from the shedding of innocent blood, and restricted their share in the reign of terror which had now commenced to a moral support of the atrocious crimes perpetrated under the cloak of religious zeal by the privileged classes for the practical subversion of the legitimate monarchy, and the consequent perpetuation of their own political and spiritual supremacy.

That incomparable villain, Titus Oates—the honoured pensioner of William III.—on being summoned to the bar of the Lower House, declared that the Pope had assumed the sovereignty of the British Isles, and had delegated his authority to the Jesuits; that the general of that order had already appointed a Government of Catholic noblemen and gentlemen whom he named, and had bestowed the dignities and benefices of the Anglican Church on foreign as well as native Romanists; that the Jesuits were raising up a French party to overthrow the Prince of Orange in Holland, and were fomenting revolution in Ireland and Scotland; while in England they had not only decreed the massacre of the leading nobility and gentry, but also the assassination of the King, and the elevation to the throne of the Duke of York as the Pope's vassal. And a subsequent informer—the oft-convicted swindler and impostor, William Bedloe—invested the marvellous Plot with new horrors, by declaring that French and Spanish armies—France and Spain being at that very time engaged in mutual slaughter — were to be landed in England, and after effecting a junction with the native forces raised by the Catholic lords, were to fire London, commence a general massacre of the Protestants throughout the kingdom, and, should the Duke of York prove refractory, place the government in the hands of a committee of noblemen appointed by the Pope. Archbishop Sheldon—the blackest and most odious type of Anglican prelacy—whose persecutions were merely political, and "who considered religion chiefly as an engine of policy," fanned the flame of popular bigotry and fanaticism. And the Church staunchly seconded the efforts of its primate. "None," says Hallam, " none had more contributed to raise the national outcry against the accused, and create a firm persuasion of the reality of the Plot, than the clergy in their sermons, even the most respectable of their order, Sancroft, Sharp, Barlow, Burnet, Tillotson, Stillingfleet ; inferring its truth from Godfrey's murder and Coleman's letter, calling for the severest laws against the Catholics, and imputing to them the fire of London—nay, even the death of Charles I." Both Houses of Parliament, also affecting to believe in the horrid imposture, proclaim a solemn fast, ordain a special form of prayer to be contrived for the occasion, and vote unanimously : " That there is and hath been a damnable and hellish plot, contrived and carried out by Popish recusants, for assassinating and murdering the King, for subverting the Government, and rooting out and destroying the Protestant religion." They represent to Charles that their paramount duty is "to endeavour by the most speedy and effectual means the suppression of Popery within this your kingdom, and the bringing to public justice all such as shall be found guilty of the horrid and damnable Popish Plot." And in a subsequent address they pray : " That His Majesty would be pleased to order the execution of one Pickering, a prisoner in

Newgate, and of divers priests and Jesuits, who had been condemned by the judges at the Old Bailey, and in the several Circuits; to the great emboldening of such offenders, in case they should escape without due punishment." Terrorized by the Cavalier Parliament, the horrified King—who in private denounced and ridiculed the gross imposture, saying that "he was accused of being in a plot against his own life,"—was nevertheless constrained for the preservation of that life to become the reluctant instrument of their will. The Catholic lords were at once thrown into the Tower, and two thousand of their co-religionists into the various gaols of the metropolis. One proclamation banished all Catholics from London, another ordered their arrest throughout the kingdom. The abused nation was beside itself with fear and rage. In the capital the train-bands and volunteers were under arms night and day, patrols paraded the streets, batteries were planted at Whitehall, and barricades erected in all the leading thoroughfares, in expectation of the predicted Catholic rising. The fermentation spread to the remotest districts of the kingdom, and every centre of population presented in miniature the humiliating spectacle of the metropolis. At the same time the mob was enlisted in the service of the caste. The chronic, and in the main, the unfounded jealousy and dread of Romanism entertained by the populace since the Reformation, had always been a potent force in politics, and had been often used by the aristocracy and Church as a means for the attainment of their selfish purposes ; but never was it so unscrupulously and triumphantly brought into operation as during their long, and—but for their canting party-cry—their utterly hopeless, nay, impossible struggle with Charles and James for the absolute sovereignty of the British Isles. Reared systematically by Anglicanism in a state of the grossest ignorance, and abused with the wildest views and calumnies of Romanism, the masses were now easily deluded by an unprincipled and designing caste into the insane belief that a Popish knife menaced every Protestant throat ; and were led to participate in a series of cowardly and bloody excesses, which were quite alien to the national character, and which in all human probability will ever form the darkest scenes in our history. Misled by their hereditary masters, they clamour for the blood of the

Catholics, and, thronging the courts of law, maltreat the witnesses of the accused, greet with roars of applause their unjust condemnation, and, with eager step and fierce yells of rage and execration, follow them to the gallows. Convicted on the false testimony of the basest of mankind of conspiring the death of the King, the subversion of the Government, and the destruction of the Protestant religion as by law established in the Church of England, batches of unhappy victims were hanged, drawn, and quartered, all protesting before God, with their last breath, that they were wholly innocent of the crimes laid to their charge, and for which, amidst such black and brutal surroundings, they suffered the awful doom of traitors.

Meanwhile the Cavalier Parliament, which had stuck at no crime to raise the popular tempest, hastened to turn it to account. The atrocious statute of the reign of Elizabeth, ordering all native Catholic clergymen to leave the kingdom within the space of forty days, on pain of death, was again declared to be in force. The Parliamentary Test Act—which was not repealed till 1828—was hurriedly passed, without opposition, disabling Puritans as well as Papists from sitting in either House of Parliament or holding any office, civil or military, under the Crown. The Duke of York was forced to seek refuge in Flanders. The Queen herself was accused of having said to a party of Jesuits, within earshot of Oates, who lay concealed behind an open door, that in revenge for the infidelities of her husband " I will join in his death and the propagation of the Catholic faith ! " And, drunk with the audacity and villainy of his aristocratic accomplices, that perjured monster, as hideous in person as in character, appears at the bar of the House of Lords and in blatant tones impeaches " Catherine, Queen of England, of high treason." Hereupon the Cavalier Parliament present an address to the King praying that the Queen and her domestics might be at once removed from Whitehall. "The villains," exclaimed the indignant and outraged monarch, " the villains think I have a mind for a new wife ; but, for all that, they shall see I will not allow an innocent woman to be abused." He assures the terrified Queen of his protection, and orders her vile calumniator—who he knew was tutored in his base and bloody work—to be placed under arrest and kept in close seclusion. But the Cavalier Parliament, conscious that these restrictions would be fatal to the Plot, immediately force the King not simply to release their infamous but invaluable associate, whom they impiously declare "the saviour of his country," but to grant him a generous pension and apartments in the palace of Whitehall, and a special guard to protect him from Popish assassins. They next proceed to attack the King himself for having made an application to the Court of France for the same disgraceful pecuniary aid which they themselves, without excuse, had been receiving, and which had won for them the epithet of the Pension Parliament, when their existence was suddenly cut short by a dissolution A.D. 1678.

Thus perished abruptly, under circumstances of peculiar and unexampled infamy, the Cavalier or Pension Parliament, after a prolonged existence of nearly eighteen years. Its mission, however, had been fully accomplished. The offspring and delegate of the vanquished descendants of our Norman Conquerors, whom Monk had rescued from political shipwreck and restored, in all their pristine strength and splendour, to their ancient proud preeminence, the Cavalier Parliament had reestablished on a legal basis the old Norman domination which the Republic had supplanted after six centuries of tyranny and oppression. But in its work of reconstruction it had introduced such momentous changes in the revived political and religious system of the Norman Conquest as practically to strip the Crown of all real power so far as the internal government of the country was concerned, and to establish, by the enactment of such "solid and lasting provisions" against all future democratic revolutions as the Corporation Act, the Act of Uniformity, the Conventicle, Five Mile Test, and Parliamentary Test Acts, the despotism and tyranny of the aristocracy and Church. In a word, the Cavalier Parliament, placing both King and people at its feet, transmitted to succeeding Parliaments, elected almost exclusively by, and composed almost entirely of, hereditary property and rank, a legal title to arbitrary power which the territorial families—forewarned by their dismal fate under the Commonwealth—would never voluntarily abdicate, and of which they could never be deprived but by a violation of their strangely reconstructed Constitution in Church and State; and on the altar of their atrocious laws—as they doubted its continued loyalty to their vast and permanent conspiracy against the nation whom they evermore distrusted—the aristocracy and Church still resolved to immolate the Norman dynasty of the Stuarts.

Thrice did the King—in the hope of securing the return of a House less hostile to the legitimate and national monarchy, which was now the only obstacle and check to caste despotism — summon new Parliaments; but elected practically by the nobility, clergy, and gentry, they were composed of almost entirely the same members and advocated the same policy. Each successive Parliament—in close communication with the Prince of Orange, who, with the basest motives, entered deeply into all their intrigues, encouraged their wildest excesses, and at the same time, by his secret emissaries, kept alive the popular panic—were alike bent on the perpetuation of their reign of terror till they had forced the King to disinherit his brother by the passage of the Bill of Exclusion. At their instigation the Prince urges on the King the advisability of submission to the will of Parliament, and the States-General of Holland, through Pensionary Fagel invite Charles, without delay, not simply to sacrifice his brother to the ambitious designs of their stadtholder, but England itself to the military requirements of Holland. But King Charles, standing alone in his realm—as on a previous occasion he had told King Louis—resists all pressure, foreign as well as domestic. He saw that the tide of popular frenzy was on the turn, that the mob was sated with innocent blood, and that his triumph was at hand. For nearly two years had this reign of terror lasted, during which period of time the lives of the Catholics, and of the Royal Family itself, were literally at the mercy of Anglicanism and of its instruments and dupes, the treacherous and perjured informer, and the illiterate and brutal mob; but the general belief in the monstrous Plot had been solely kept alive by the foulest judicial murders. And the execution of the Earl of Stafford—after a lengthened trial by the House of Peers—who, like the less noble victims of the Popish Plot, died protesting his innocence of the crimes for which he was condemned, and expressing the hope that the delusion of which he was the victim would soon pass away, and the stigma cast on his name would be speedily effaced—at length opened the eyes of the masses to the snare into which they had been entrapped. They now regarded with shame and remorse the horrors in which they had blindly participated, and with indignation and abhorrence the malignant factions which had wilfully deluded them. And the King shared the fierce resentment and poignant sorrow of the multitude. "The Queen Consort," writes Terriesi, the Tuscan Minister in London, "the Queen Consort affirms that he never came into her private cabinet where she kept, after their execution, the portraits of the Jesuits who were massacred in that false conspiracy, without turning towards them and kissing their hands, and asking their pardon in the humblest and most penitent form, without dilating passionately on his own guilt and on their innocence, concluding with the remark that they were now in a place where they could truly know whether His Majesty had been forced to act as he did, and entreating that they would pray God on his behalf to pardon the offence" (A.D. 1681). And in this frame of mind King Charles, taking advantage of the sudden revulsion of popular sentiment, dissolves his fifth and last Parliament, and appeals in a royal manifesto to the nation to judge between him and them, whom he accuses of insisting on the exclusion of his brother from the succession, notwithstanding all the remedies he had proposed for the security of the Anglican Church; and of forbidding anyone to lend him money, in the hope that his financial needs would constrain him to a servile compliance with their will; in a word, of endeavouring by the most unwarrantable and seditious means to establish their own arbitrary power—which they had indeed by law effected—on the ruins of the Monarchy. The Declaration was received with the liveliest demonstrations of loyalty by the people, who rejoiced at the emancipation of their sovereign from aristocratic tyranny. And the King, whose easy and clement disposition was observed to change very visibly, and to become cruel and vindictive, owing to the countless indignities and dangers he had undergone, thirsting to avenge the innocent blood he had been compelled to shed, enlists the gang of perjurers who had sworn away the lives of the Catholics into his own service, and thinking that no retaliation on opponents so steeped in infamy could be unjust, turns this vile weapon with deadly effect against its late employers.

Then was witnessed one of those political changes of front and general abandonment of so-called principles, which were characteristic of our governing classes in the presence of overwhelming danger. It is true that they had already nominally divided into two hostile parties, the one favouring and the other opposing an unlimited royal prerogative; but in reality one and indivisible in origin and interest, the Whigs and Tories have never failed to coalesce—since their dismal overthrow by Oliver Cromwell—whenever danger from whatsoever quarter menaced the sovereignty of their common order. And now recognizing the peril of a prolongation of their struggle with King Charles, supported by the multitude, the vast majority of the nobility and landed gentry, with the whole body of the clergy, hushing their sinister and immoral cry of "No Popery," which for the nonce had lost its ancient potency, rally with an outburst of sham loyalty round that Norman throne they had erewhile so vilely sought to seize and fill with a foreign puppet of their own selection.

The Declaration of the King was read in all the churches. And the clergy who had been hitherto the chief supporters of the Popish

Plot—assured of the King's protection—again elevate the doctrines of passive obedience and non-resistance into articles of religion, and denounce eternal punishments against all who dare resist "the Lord's anointed and the ministers of the only true Church upon earth."

And the Prince of Orange shared, in his own person, the discomfiture of his partisans. At this crisis of his and England's fortunes, with the audacity of a born conspirator and revolutionist, he came to England on the pretence of inducing Charles to adopt his continental policy, but in reality to ascertain the strength of the Exclusionists, to revive their drooping courage, and renew by personal intercourse his miserable intrigues with them. And Monmouth—never a serious rival—with the other leaders of the dwindling Whigs— soon for a time to be discredited and ruined by their participation in the murderous Rye House Plot—hasten to court their eagerly responsive Dutch protector, panting as ever to seize by any means his uncle's crown, and, for his personal glory and aggrandizement, to embroil the English nation with the French. To hasten and facilitate the accomplishment of this vast design, his aim had ever been to alarm, to link together, and direct all menaced interests, the petty privileges and properties of the Corporation cliques, together with the mighty political and social forces of hereditary property and rank. In a word, he decreed that the corporations of the towns —those bribes and sops of the astute Norman to the wealthier section of the conquered race—should march side by side with the Norman baronage, landed gentry, and the Church under his all-protecting banner. But his tampering with the Corporation of the city, with whom he dined immediately on reaching London, and his ostentatious conferences with the wrecks of the defeated faction remaining steadfast to their nefarious Popish Plot imposture—whose chief contriver, Titus Oates, he subsequently patronized and pensioned—at length aroused the disgust and indignation of the Court, and brought to a somewhat abrupt close his brief but sinister visitation.

A.D. 1682-1685.—But the so-called second tyranny of the Stuarts was in reality the unbridled reign of caste ferocity. The King indeed, dispensed with Parliaments, but their atrocious laws were in full force. And the haughty and implacable caste, living in constant dread of the democracy, who, in their judgment, could be only held in due subjection by the rigorous enforcement of the repressive legislation provided for that purpose, exacted from the King, as the price of their reviving loyalty, the gratification—under the old disguise of fierce religious persecution—of their unslaked vengeance on their late plebeian conquerors. Nay, more, with unparalleled effrontery they cast upon the Dissenters—whom, in order to estrange from the Court, they had, by foully slandering the Catholics, ensnared into a passive participation in their own detestable imposture—the whole odium of the Popish Plot, branding them, in a multitude of addresses to the King, with the vile epithets of rebels and villains. Yet King Charles, whose priniciple and practice it had ever been to free the consciences of all his subjects, again mildly makes mention of a proposal for the renewal of the Indulgence to Nonconformists; which had, however, immediately to be withdrawn in deference to the contemptuous opposition of the caste, who denounce all Puritans as the professed enemies of the King, the Church, and State. And during the remainder of his reign the gaols were crammed to overflowing with hosts of unnumbered martyrs, of whom four thousand alone belonged to the petty sect of grave and peaceful Quakers. He died rejecting the religion of the sycophantic and persecuting prelates who hung about his bed, craving to share his dying blessing with his mistresses.

The nobler features of his character—obscured by glaring personal vices—he shall himself portray. Under the shadow of the Republic, and as a barrier against its imminent restoration, he had consented to those odious laws which virtually enslaved his people and himself. Too late, he realizes the momentous consequences of his, perhaps, involuntary act, and standing alone in his realm — misrepresented and maligned — he did all that a single arm could safely do to rescue the disarmed multitude from the persecuting and revengeful fury of their hereditary and legally constituted tyrants and masters. "Though such laws have been made, I am against persecution, and I hope soon to stand on my own legs, and then you shall see how much I am against," was his reply to a deputation of Dissenting ministers, who recognized in him their sole protector. "I have always been tender in matters of blood, which my subjects have no reason to take exception at; I shall, therefore, consider it, and return you an answer," was his rebuke to an address of the Cavalier Parliament clamouring for the instant execution of innocent men, falsely condemned as Popish Plot conspirators. When the caste, through their mouthpiece, the Cavalier Parliament, urged him to draw the sword of England in defence of purely Dutch and German interests, he resolutely refused. "This kingdom," said he, "this kingdom must necessarily own the vast advantage it has received by peace, whilst its neighbours only have yet smarted by the war." In a word, like his gallant grandsire, Henry of Navarre, King Charles the Second had a "great clemency and tenderness to his people," and forswearing his alliance with the privileged classes, when he perceived that, having fettered the democracy, they were still insatiate of sheer revenge on their late plebeian conquerors, he risked his crown—in spite of their occasional estrangement from him through the mendacities and slanders of their common enemies, who feared their coalition—vainly endeavouring to deliver them from persecution. And though he failed to permanently mitigate the ferocity of legislation which his and their enemies thought necessary for the maintenance of the Restoration system, yet in defiance of the aristocracy, the Church, and their Dutch ally, King Charles the Second saved England—and that is his lasting title to our gratitude—from the untold horrors of wanton Continental warfare.

In Scotland, prelacy was guilty of still more atrocious barbarities on the Covenanters. There an entire nation had to be reduced to the yoke of episcopacy, and to an army was entrusted the task of the conversion. The thumb-screw, the rack, and the iron-boot were called into constant requisition as adjuncts to that army. And the unique mission of the brutal and semi-savage soldiery of Turner, Dalziel, and Claverhouse was to hunt down and imprison, or to torture and massacre, at their will, the fugitive martyrs. It was not a persecution in the ordinary acceptation of the phrase, but rather the proscription of the whole Scottish people of the Lowlands. Multitudes of the Covenanters were transported as slaves to America. But ere they quitted their native land, episcopacy set its fell brand upon them. Many of the men were mutilated, and the women were burnt on the cheek with a hot iron. A detail of those barbarities would "harrow up the soul" and freeze the blood of the most callous-hearted; but the subject is too repulsive, too heart-rending to dwell upon. It will be sufficient to state that the cruelties inflicted on the Covenanters have stamped that era of Scottish history as emphatically the time of persecution. Thus did the lords and lairds of the Drunken Parliament and its successors avenge on the democracy their brief exclusion from power under the Commonwealth.

In Ireland, Anglicanism was ever synonymous with injustice and tyranny; for the greater portion of its soil had been confiscated, and the revenues of its ancient and National Church had been alienated since the Reformation. There, it was a political organization pure and simple, and affected no pretensions to a sacred mission beyond the pale of its immediate supporters—the Anglo-Irish colonists and conquerors. So far indeed was it from attempting the evangelization of the Celtic population, that its clergy were incapable even of speaking the Erse tongue, and were in reality but sinecurists, who held their benefices by virtue of social and political influences. Irish Anglicanism was the symbol of the most atrocious despotism which has perhaps ever existed in a civilized community to desolate and shock mankind. It ever went hand-in-hand with the secular power in the interminable wars of extermination which were waged against the religion and race of Ireland. It was the incarnation of that inhuman policy which had for years harried the Celts to insurrection, that it might confiscate their lands; in a word of a policy whose unique object was the utter annihilation of the Celtic race. The Celt therefore confounded in a common hatred Protestantism and the English race—the Anglican Church and foreign oppression. Popery was to him the symbol of independence, the Romish priest was to him a brother in blood and faith, but the bishops and clergymen of the Established Church—aliens alike in race and sentiment, and members of a persecuting priesthood—were to him the worst embodiment and type of foreign domination. Yet this garrison Church of the conquerors was, until recently, with an injustice at once grotesque and insulting, called the National Church, and was imposed on the conquered as a badge at once of their spiritual as well as temporal servitude.

Moreover—and here I must be guilty of a brief digression—Anglicanism has intensified the mutual animosities of the rival races who people Ireland, and its spiritual laches have undoubtedly contributed to the perpetuation of the Roman Catholic religion there. Well had it been for Ireland had the extermination of Popery been accomplished at the time of the Reformation. I believe it to be that country's greatest curse. I believe that we may attribute to it most of the poverty and crime which so rankly flourish there. I believe that were Ireland twenty times as large and twenty times as fertile as it is at this moment, that the same misery and poverty would exist so long as the Romish priest exercised his baneful influence over the consciences of the ignorant, and therefore credulous and superstitious inhabitants, an influence which destroys all individual self-reliance, all freewill of action, the indispensable conditions for material success all the world over. My experience of a section of the Celtic Irish Romanists in America has forced these convictions on me. One would have thought that poverty in Texas and

Louisiana would have been utterly impossible, and that there the Irish Celt would have been in his glory. But alas! what to my astonishment was the condition in which, to a great extent, I found him? It is the same old, old tale. I found the same poverty, the same dirt, the same rags, and last of all, and the cause of all, the same ignorance and superstition, that so often pain the sight, and heart too, of a stranger in Ireland. Such is my general personal experience of the Celtic Irish Romanist in Louisiana and Texas. Ask any American northerner or southerner and he will tell you as his experience, that all the material advantages of his great country will avail the Celt little or nothing, so long as his conscience is fettered by the bonds of Romish priestcraft. But let the scales of superstition drop from his eyes, let him put his trust in his God and in his own right arm, instead of in his priest, and you will see him march with the foremost of any nation to assured success, and his children will become great in the land of his adoption.

You will ask then: "What remedy, what antidote is there for this incubus Popery—this admitted curse of the Irish race?" My reply is, Justice on our part to the downtrodden Celts.

For whilst it is an indisputable, nay a notorious fact to those who have lived in the United States, that most of the adult Irish emigrants live and die in the religion in which they were born and bred, and suffer throughout their whole lives from the evil effects of its teaching, it should be distinctly remembered that it is at the same time equally indisputable and notorious that, in perhaps the majority of cases, the descendants of these emigrants renounce altogether the religion of their fathers. You will ask then why it is they cling so tenaciously to the Romish superstition in their own country? And I will answer you frankly even at the risk of offending your national prejudices. I will endeavour to state the case from an Irish, or rather Celtic point of view. They cling to Romanism partially because of ignorance; because its priesthood is Celtic, that is to say national; because it is, or rather has been, a politically persecuted church; but I aver chiefly because they believe that a religion which permits one nation to oppress another as England, or rather the aristocracy of England, has oppressed Ireland, must necessarily be false.

You will ask: "In what consists this oppression?" My reply is briefly this. The population of Ireland, as you know, is composed of two distinct races, the Celts or aborigines and the Anglo-Irish, between whom there is as wide a gulf as divers religions and origin, and seven centuries of hostility can create. The Celts number nearly four millions and the Anglo-Irish about one million and a half. The latter possess thirteen-fourteenths of the soil, which has been wrested from the Celts, not at one fell swoop at the Norman Conquest of Ireland in 1169, but piecemeal, extending over nearly seven centuries of time. The later great confiscations of land under James I., Cromwell, William III., and even under George III., are so comparatively recent as to be still fresh in the Celtic mind, and by their very freshness they reopen the whole history of their struggles with their conquerors. The whole aristocracy of Ireland are with a very few exceptions of the conquering race. The administration of justice, together with every office of power, trust, or emolument, is with comparatively speaking few exceptions also in the hands of the conquerors. Finally the policy of the British Government, and especially of the Anglo-Irish landlords, has been, to root out of the soil and to expatriate the native Celts, whom they have dispossessed of their lands, and so successfully has this inhuman policy been carried out, that the native Celtic population, within the last forty years, has decreased from seven and a quarter to less than four millions.

And what has been the result of a policy by which the entire Celtic race has been deliberately and systematically sacrificed to ten or twenty thousand, more or less, Anglo-Irish landlords and English noblemen? The most natural result in the world. The Celtic Irish are disloyal almost to a man, and the British Government has generally found it necessary to govern Ireland by the bayonet of the soldier, the musket of the policeman, and the treacherous lie of the informer. Such is the condition of the native Irish, and that of the stranger is scarcely better. Every Englishman who sets foot on a proclaimed district in Ireland is at once subject to the surveillance of the police, and is liable at any moment to arrest and imprisonment.

Such then is the state of Ireland, and what do you think of it? In times of peace I admit we can afford to set at defiance every principle of right and justice; but we should remember that we cannot tell what a day may bring forth; that breakers may be ahead in the shape of foreign war; and that should such be the case, we all know that it is a desperate game we are playing at, imperilling the interests, aye the very integrity of the empire.

We should do well to bear in mind a past and most disastrous page of our history, and to take warning therefrom. Some century ago, the King and aristocracy of this country endeavoured to impose an illegal tax on the Americans; they resisted, and with foreign aid defeated us; and we, with a grotesque inconsequence, have ever since belauded and exaggerated the virtues, the valour, and the cause of a people we attempted slightly to wrong, and have placed their chief, Washington, on a pinnacle of glory, unique of its kind, extolling him as a model of all the virtues.

Shall we persist in our injustice towards Ireland, until—involved in foreign war—the Celts with foreign aid throw off our yoke? and shall we then, to be consistent, exalt some Irish Washington as far above the American one as Ireland's wrongs have exceeded those of America? Or profiting by the lessons of the past, shall we hold out our hand to our Irish brethren and say: "You have helped to make this empire what it is. From Cressy and Agincourt to Candahar and Tel-el-Kebir you have fought side by side and shed your blood with us. We confess you have met with great injustice in the past, not at the hands of the people of England, but of the aristocracy, who have been hitherto our masters as well as yours. England, like Ireland, mourns the expatriation of her sturdiest sons, and the confiscation of her soil. But we have finally shattered our oppressors' power, and we are determined that neither race shall henceforth be sacrificed to them."

Then would Ireland, believing in your justice, and casting aside all religious and national prejudices, be prepared to receive your teaching. Justice first and above all things—but this by no means embraces the monstrous crime and blunder involved in the concession of Irish legislative independence, which would speedily entail the severance of the sacred bonds that so happily unite the Imperial Sister Islands of the West—and then, as the Romish superstition has its foundation in ignorance, flourishes in ignorance, but dies with ignorance, education will be its sovereign remedy. Ring in their ears the words and deeds of the Pilgrim Fathers; teach them the civil and religious principles of the later Puritans, principles which have made the democracy of England—under the different designations which localities have given it—the regenerating and ruling force on earth. Then I believe that—perhaps within a generation, but certainly in due course of time—the Celts of Ireland, like their brother Celts of Scotland, Wales, and Cornwall, will become as intensely Protestant as they are now passionately Roman Catholic.

We all know, and none of us better than those who have lived in Roman Catholic countries, that the Church of Rome, as a religious system, has no real vitality in it. Its vitality is like the artificial vitality of the galvanized corpse, which moves, which has an apparent life—but

> "Its bones are marrowless, its blood is cold,
>   There is no speculation in those eyes
>   That it doth glare with!"

Still this Church is a political necessity to the despotisms of the Continent. For the Romish priests—who are but the tools of the governments, and who preach as a religious dogma, passive obedience to the powers that be—keep the weak-minded and ignorant classes of those countries in subjection by the dread of the eternal punishments they denounce against all who dare resist their tyrants, whom they style the Lord's anointed. And in order to maintain this state of things, the crowned despots of the Continent uphold with all their moral might that "Triple Tyrant" the Pope, whose power without such aid would in an instant,

> "Like the baseless fabric of a vision,
> Fade and dissolve away."

I believe that a round unvarnished history of the Roman Church would of itself be sufficient to make any man, who has the heart and blood of a man, shrink with horror from contact with that unholy, that accursed thing.

Educate, then, I say, and the Romish superstition will die. Then will Ireland be not only the "Gem of Ocean," as the Irish delight to call her, but the home of a free, contented, and prosperous, because a united people, united by the strongest of all bonds, the bonds of a common, a holy faith.

In Wales, Anglicanism had ever been a negative rather than a positive curse. There the hierarchy—being also sinecurists, and almost to a man strangers—were incapable, had they been disposed, of preaching the gospel to the Welsh. And so appalling and complete was the state of spiritual darkness and destitution which prevailed in Wales, owing to this culpable neglect, that prior to 1804 but few Bibles in the native tongue were to be found throughout the principality. Heathenism had perhaps resumed its sway in Wales, had not honest men been raised up to prick the conscience of a slumbering nation, and to shame to an artificial exertion, by their noble example, a section of that recreant priesthood who had been traitors alike to their God, their conscience, and their country.

V.

BETRAYAL OF ENGLAND AND THE NORMAN LINE

INTO THE HANDS OF THE DUTCH INVADERS, BY THE NOBILITY, CLERGY, AND GENTRY.

A.D. 1685-1688. We have traced the distinctive characteristics of Anglicanism in England and Scotland to the reign of Charles II., and in Ireland and Wales to our own times. We shall now resume the consideration of the History of the Church in Great Britain. Towards the close of the reign of the Merry Monarch, as the Anglicans have complacently styled King Charles II., the Universities—those thrones of Anglicanism and nurseries of caste—fired with mutual emulation, profess and teach, in singular perspicuity of terms, the most despotic principles. The University of Cambridge, through its Vice-Chancellor, addressed the King in the following terms: "We will still believe and maintain, That our kings derive not their titles from the People, but from God: That to him alone they are accountable: That it belongs not to subjects, either to create or censure, but to honour and obey their sovereign, who comes to be so, by a fundamental hereditary right of succession, which no religion, no law, no fault or forfeiture can alter or diminish." And on the very day of Lord Russell's execution, the University of Oxford, in enunciating the same well-known axioms, had somewhat superfluously declared, "submission and obedience—clear, absolute and without exception—to be the badge and character of the Church of England." And its absolute subserviency to the capricious will of its royal masters had been hitherto never—save during the Popish Plot commotion—called into question, and was a fact of historical notoriety. But we now approach the period when, touched in its own interests, it became false to the doctrine which gave it existence, and a traitor to its supreme temporal head. The Romish James had now ascended the throne, and so long as he assented to their atrocious persecution of his Dissenting subjects, the nobility, clergy, and gentry were his partisans and abettors. They had combated to a man the rising of the deluded democrats under Monmouth, and after its merciless suppression, a section of them had shocked even the brutal Jeffries by their indecent scramble for the prisoners, who were to be sold as slaves in America. But no sooner did James manifest an intention to dispense with and suspend the odious laws on which their own despotism was founded, and possibly to revindicate the rights of the old Roman Church to their detriment, than the rich and powerful Anglican episcopacy—with its supporters and patrons, the temporal peers and landed gentry, the inheritors of the ancient abbey lands—plotted his ruin. Fearing to rely on the English nation, which might in the throes of a popular revolution have again taken the management of affairs into its own hands, they resolved to invite into the country a foreign army, and by its means effect a revolution which should maintain and perpetuate their menaced monopoly of political and sacerdotal power. The struggle thus inaugurated was simply a revival of that miserable conflict between privilege and prerogative which had been brought to a close towards the end of the reign of Charles II. Court and caste again fight for supremacy over the prostrate body of a despised nation, which was in turn the prey and dupe of either successful combatant. Both were discredited by sinister antecedents. The unspeakable horrors of the Popish Plot, and the barbarities which for a quarter of a century had desolated the homes of Dissent—or rather the homes of the betrayed democracy of Puritanic England—had branded the caste with eternal infamy; whilst James's persecution of the Covenanters—although political rather than religious—was a ghastly comment on his zeal for freedom of conscience. Both were bespattered with blood of Sedgemoor, and of the victims of Kirke and Jeffries. The battle-cry of either was a specious, yet false utterance. But the caste asserted its right to pre-eminence in political crime, and crowned its double treason by a standing conspiracy with the foreigner, on whom it relied for final victory.

I cannot sympathise with either of these warring elements—both noxious in their origin and essence—but of the two great rival evils James was certainly the lesser one.

Moreover, the Stuart King possessed one supreme virtue which his adversaries lacked—a true, if misdirected patriotism, that would at least have shielded England from wanton warfare and dismemberment.

"I think it fit," says he, addressing his Privy Council within an hour of his brother's death, "I think it fit to declare to you that I will endeavour to follow his example, and most especially in that of his great clemency and tenderness to his people." "I have," said he, addressing his Parliament, "I have a true English heart, as jealous of the honour of the nation as you can be, and I please myself with the hopes that, by God's blessing and your assistance, I shall carry the reputation of it yet higher in the world than ever it has been in the time of any of my ancestors." And on another occasion he said: "Our chief aim has been not to be the oppressor, but the father of our people." And yet again, "I will venture even my life in defence of the true interest of this kingdom." And when threatened with Dutch invasion, he repeatedly rejects the offer of French armed assistance, declaring to his people: "Although I have had notice for some time since that a foreign force was preparing against me, yet I have always declined any foreign succours; but rather have chosen, next under God, to rely upon the true and ancient courage, faith and allegiance of my own people." And after his dethronement, when none could doubt the sincerity of his language, he refused the aid of an overwhelming French force for the reconquest of his lost kingdoms, saying: "He did not choose to owe his restoration to foreigners, but to his own friends." And at the Boyne, as he beheld the cavalry of Hamilton committing havoc in the ranks of his enemies, he was heard repeatedly to exclaim: "Oh! spare my English subjects!" And when from the beach of La Hague, and under fire of the English flotilla—indeed, the horse of the bailiff of Montebourg, who was by the side of King James, had its leg broken by a musket shot from one of the gunboats—he witnessed the destruction of the French fleet, and with it his last hope of restoration, he could not refrain from expressing his admiration of the valour and conduct of those gallant seamen, whom in happier days he had styled "the strength and glory of this nation," and whom he had so often led to victory. "None but my brave English tars could have done this!"

cried the dethroned monarch, proudly, as Rooke wrapped in flames the mighty three-deckers of De Tourville.

During the late reign James had urged the King to a life and death struggle for the overthrow of the despotic caste, but Charles, recognizing the hopeless character of such an unequal contest, had wisely declined to follow the leading of his reckless brother. "You may, if you like, set out on your travels again, but I am too old to stir, and shall remain where I am," the King, it was reported, had been overheard to say to the Duke. Yet James, with a simplicity peculiar to himself, hopes to induce his Parliament, composed of monarchical Church of England men, to repeal voluntarily the Test and Penal Laws which had legalized the Restoration of the ancient domination founded by the Norman Duke, of which Anglicanism was the eternal spiritual symbol, and its abolition the immediate signal of democratic revolution. With this object in view, he had recourse to an expedient which he trusted would overcome all opposition. The leading members of both Houses are summoned separately to his presence, and are entreated —as a personal obligation to their monarch—

to vote for the repeal of the repressive legislation of the Cavalier Parliament; in other words, to set at liberty the hosts of Puritans and Catholics, who for conscience' sake tenanted, with thieves and cut-throats, the gaols of England; and to throw open the parliament, the public services, and the universities to their countrymen of all denominations. Whilst James was closeted at Whitehall with the legislators in town, the judges, then on circuit, summoned to the different county towns the members in the country, and made to them, on behalf of the King, the same proposals. But the aristocracy and Church—who had been commissioned by King Charles II. " to provide after so many and great revolutions, proper remedies for those evils, and to prevent the like for the future," and who, in eager execution of the royal mandate, had, under the shadow and in terror of the Republic, passed in rapid succession the Corporation Act, the Act of Uniformity, the Conventicle, Five Mile, Test, and Parliamentary Test Acts, as lasting and impregnable barriers against the democracy, which, under the guidance of the invincible Oliver, had conquered them, and from whose capacious jaws the powerful arm of the traitor Monk alone has rescued them—scouting their repeal as an act of political suicide, bluntly refuse to accede to the wishes of the King, whose new form of appeal to their loyalty and patriotism they ridicule as private lecturings, tamperings, and mean closetings. We have already seen how the nobility, clergy, and gentry had, by their practical political annihilation of both the democracy and crown, become the depositories of all power; how they had established, with loudest protestations of loyalty, that worst of all tyrannies, the absolute domination of a restored and vindictive caste of conquerors, destitute alike of individual conscience and responsibility; how, filled with a permanent distrust and dread of their late plebeian masters, they had with all due forms of law again enslaved the nation; how, strong in their dark and permanent conspiracy with the Prince of Orange and the Dutch, they had striven to overawe and crush the recalcitrant Court by the exclusion, on the flimsiest of pretexts, of the Duke of York from the succession, heaping on his devoted head all the monstrous and impossible crimes attributed to the Papists by the infamous contrivers of the Popish Plot. And we now behold them confronting their King with haughty defiance, and answering his appeal for mercy on his subjects, with fiercer outrages. At their command the persecution, which had abated since the death of Charles II., was renewed with redoubled violence. Every Dissenting chapel was closed, and every conventicle dispersed. The gaols could not contain the multitude of martyrs. Yet the pulpits of the Church, which perpetrated these horrors, resounded with the wildest and fiercest denunciations of the Catholics, and by implication, of the King their co-religionist and head. After enduring this virulent abuse and persecution for two years, James's patience was quite exhausted. And fortified by the opinions of the judges in favour of a dispensing power, he resolved to shatter at a blow the despotism of the privileged classes by the abrogation of the terrible laws which were its sanction and foundation.

A.D. 1687.—Accordingly he told his Privy Council he had been led to take this step from having observed, "That although an uniformity in religious worship had been endeavoured to be established within this kingdom in the successive reigns of four of his predecessors, assisted by their respective parliaments, yet it had proved altogether ineffectual. That the restraint upon the consciences of Dissenters, in order thereunto had been very prejudicial to the nation, as was sadly experienced by the horrid rebellion in the time of His Majesty's father. That the many penal laws made against Dissenters had rather increased than lessened the numbers of them. And that nothing could more conduce to the peace" and prosperity " of this kingdom," or be more in accordance " with the principles of Christianity, than an entire liberty of conscience." And in pursuance of this speech, King James issued, on the 4th of April, 1687, his celebrated Declaration of Indulgence, which, like the testament of Edward the Confessor, in favour of William the Conqueror, was made the pretext for a foreign invasion, attended with consequences more momentous, vast, and durable than those of any event recorded in our history since the Norman Conquest.

After briefly referring to the difficulties which preceded and followed his accession to the throne, and to his desire to reign in the hearts of his people, the King expresses his regret that they and he were not members of the same Church: " yet," continues James, " we humbly thank Almighty God, it is, and hath of long time been our constant sense and opinion (which upon divers occasions we have declared) that conscience ought not to be constrained, nor people forced in matters of mere religion: It has ever been directly contrary to our inclination, is injurious to the trade and growth of nations as we think it is to the interest of government, which it destroys by spoiling trade, depopulating countries, and discouraging strangers; and finally that it never obtained the end for which it was employed. And in this we are the more confirmed by the reflections we have made upon the conduct of the four last reigns: For after all the frequent and pressing endeavours that were used in each of them to reduce this kingdom to an exact uniformity in religion, it is visible that the success has not answered the design, and that the difficulty is invincible." Therefore the King by virtue of his royal prerogative—making no doubt of the final concurrence of Parliament—suspends the execution of all penal laws in matters ecclesiastical, and freely grants to all his subjects "leave to meet and serve God after their own way and manner, be it in private houses, or places purposely hired or built for that use." "And forasmuch," proceeds the Declaration, "as we are desirous to have the benefit of the service of all our loving subjects, which by the law of nature is inseparably annexed to, and inherent in our royal person; and that none of our subjects may, for the future, be under any discouragement or disability (who are otherwise well-inclined, and fit to serve us) by means of some Oaths or Tests that have been usually administered on such occasions; we do hereby further declare, that it is our royal will and pleasure, that the Oaths commonly called the Oaths of Supremacy and Allegiance, and also the several Tests and Declarations mentioned in the Acts of Parliament made in the 25th and 30th years of the reign of our late royal brother King Charles the Second; shall not at any time hereafter be required to be taken, declared or subscribed by any person or persons whatsoever, who is or shall be employed in any office or place of trust, either civil or military, under us or in our Government." "And we do further declare it to be our pleasure and intention, from time to time hereafter, to grant our royal Dispensations under our great seal, to all our loving subjects so to be employed, who shall not take the said Oaths or subscribe or declare the said Tests or Declarations in the above-mentioned Acts, and every of them."

At the same time the King guaranteed to the clergy and laity of the Anglican Church the full and entire possession of all their privileges and properties, including both the Church and abbey lands; but he destroyed their political and ecclesiastical supremacy, took from them the right to brand and butcher their fellow-countrymen, in order, from purely political motives, to establish religious uniformity, and set free the unnumbered host of Puritan martyrs—in whose ranks, we know, there were twelve hundred members of the petty sect of Quakers—whom they had thrust into their pestilential gaols with criminals of every grade of villainy.

We all know that, had King James consented to remain at the head of their vast conspiracy against the nation, the nobility, clergy, and gentry would have readily assented to any system of religion or foreign policy he might have chosen to adopt; but, perceiving that he was determined to free his people and himself from their civil and religious tyranny and oppression, they resolved with foreign bayonets to dethrone him, and their first step towards the accomplishment of this design was to reduce him to a state of utter isolation by robbing him of the hearts of his subjects. Therefore the nobility, clergy, and gentry, dreading the consequences of this attempted alliance of the King and people, close their ranks, muttering that the Declaration of Indulgence was a Jesuitical contrivance; that it was a dispensing of all the laws at once; and, as the champions of the sanctity and majesty of the law, they unfurl the banner of legality, inscribed with the names of those modern Bloody Statutes—the Corporation Act, the Act of Uniformity, the Conventicle, Five Mile, Test, and Parliamentary Test Acts—which were at once the infallible witnesses of their own triumph and of the King and nation's servitude. Nay, more. At the instigation of their Dutch Protector, whose interests were identical with their own, they declare that their bold and brutal struggle with the King for supreme domination in the British Isles was a religious war forsooth, a mortal conflict between the Anglican and Roman Churches on whose issues hung the fate of English Protestantism; and these secret confederates of the Pope and of the Catholic despots of the Continent, taking advantage of the lucky accident of the King's conversion to Catholicism and of the bigotry of the multitude whom they had reared in a state of the grossest ignorance and deluded with the wildest views of the policy of the Church of Rome, accuse the royal apostate, as they call him, of entertaining the preposterous design—having first conquered their allies, the Dutch—of enslaving and Romanizing England by means of the military power of France. Moreover, the Anglican Churches are again transformed into political arenas, and the Anglican clergy—"the most remiss of their labours in private, and the least severe in their lives" of any religious body of that age in Christendom—into unscrupulous politicians, who, trembling for their benefices, again, as at the time of the Popish Plot, attack the King through his slandered co-religionists. With marvellous yet traditional finesse the Anglican clergy divert attention from the menaced Anglican tyranny by rivetting the public gaze and concentrating the public thought upon a ghastly phantom, the weird yet grotesque offspring of their own imagination, nicknamed by them the Roman Catholic Church—which, by-the-bye, was at that very moment plotting and eagerly promoting King James's ruin and the Prince of Orange's advancement to his throne—successfully protesting from every pulpit that their close ally, the Pope, was the common enemy against whom every English Protestant must fight who would escape destruction.

But Dissenters of all denominations present addresses to the King thanking him for his Declaration of Indulgence and acknowledging in unmeasured terms his clemency and pity; and their one distinguished leader hails with enthusiasm the royal profession of a doctrine which he himself had always fondly cherished, and in defence of which had suffered long and harsh imprisonment. That illustrious personage, supreme in the history of our race for nobility of character and achievement, stands steadfast by the King. Him, whose life had been the beau ideal of Puritanic rectitude, the Anglican traitors immediately brand as a Jesuit in disguise. He was, say they, bred at St. Omer, and he received priest's orders in Rome itself. The immortal founder and lawgiver of the famous State of Pennsylvania, whose honoured name alone has saved the fair fame of their generation from total eclipse, deigns to answer his unworthy adversaries.

"If," says he, "an universal charity—if the asserting an impartial liberty of conscience—if doing to others as we would be done by, and an open avowing and steady practising of these things in all times, and to all parties, will justly lay a man under the reflection of being a Jesuit, I must not only submit to the character, but embrace it too. . . . For these are corner-stones and principles with me, and I am scandalized at all buildings which have them not for their foundations." Champions of the same cause, King James and William Penn were natural allies. "The King loved him as a singular and entire friend, and imparted to him many of his secrets and counsels. He often honoured him with his company in private, discoursing with him of various affairs, and that not for one, but many hours together, and delaying to hear the best of his peers, who were at the same time waiting for an audience." He was a constant attendant at Court, and so distinguished by royal favour that "his house and gates were daily thronged by a numerous train of clients and suppliants desiring him to present their addresses to His Majesty." Their confidence was mutual. It was the firm belief of William Penn that though

King James was himself a Romanist, he was yet a friend to religious liberty, and that he sincerely held the glorious principles he had promulgated in his Declaration of Indulgence. And the arch-quaker, as the Dutch with apprehension called him—after an abortive but sublime attempt to bring the Prince of Orange over to his views—devotes himself with unabated ardour to the great work of uniting in one powerful organization all Dissenting sects for the defence of the legitimate monarchy, by whose prerogative alone the tyranny and oppression of the privileged classes—who would never voluntarily abdicate their legal rights—could then have been subverted. But this was a task beyond the power of any single arm, and other leaders of birth and standing the Dissenters lacked, for, as we have already seen, the Puritan nobility and landed gentry, in terror of the democracy which had shattered the titled and untitled landed aristocracy, together with the Church and Throne, had at the Restoration rallied round their respective orders and the Church, adopting Anglicanism as the sacred symbol and indissoluble bond of their political unity and consequent supremacy. Moreover, the tempest of persecution, which had raged with scarcely intermittent fury ever since the Restoration, had disorganized and decimated the reeling ranks of Dissent, whilst their rigorous exclusion from the universities and public schools, and their legal deprivation of the power to educate their own children, had probably lowered the intellectual status and weakened the political and religious principles of the rising generation of Dissenters. And at the outset of his enterprise, the combined privileged classes with united voice confound in common calumny and slander both Penn and James, to thwart whose righteous purposes they tranquilly resume—in confident reliance on the intellectual darkness which since the Restoration they had striven to shed in all Dissenting homes—their ancient tactics of confusing the opinions and dividing the ranks of the Dissenters, by raising false issues and specious cries delusive of the true character of their struggle with the Court.

Meanwhile King James, blind to the universal treason of which he was the object, still set his heart on inducing the aristocracy and Church, together with their creatures the Corporation cliques, to return a Parliament pledged to the abolition of the very laws which had practically enthroned them. And it was to influence and prepare them for the ensuing general election that the King undertook in the summer of 1687 an elaborate progress—whose cardinal points were London, Portsmouth, Bath, and Chester—accompanied by his loyal follower and friend, the stainless William Penn, who, animated with the purest motives of philanthropy and patriotism, had enthusiastically embraced and championed the royal principles and cause. And hand in hand the Quaker and the King—the only powerful patrons and protectors of the multitude who thirty years before had committed the unpardonable crime of conquering the proud descendants of our Norman conquerors, and subverting the throne, Church, and baronage founded by the Norman Duke—entered, misrepresented and maligned, on their pilgrimage of mercy, to rouse a slumbering and forsaken nation, and deliver it from cruel bondage. Everywhere the public functionaries of the counties, with brilliant retinues, attended him, and vied in their official harangues with the Corporations of the towns through which he passed in wild expressions of boundless loyalty and devotion. But when in his replies the King, in conciliatory tone and language, urged—perhaps unconscious of the magnitude and bearing of the revolution he proposed—the repeal of the Test and Penal Laws, they were reserved and silent, at once perceiving, as they believed, a political abyss that was yawning at their feet, ready for the second time to engulf them. Deputations of the common people also flocked around him, and were encouraged to give utterance to the sentiments they held in common with the King. Then was witnessed the strange spectacle of the Norman monarch appealing to the multitude against the Norman aristocracy who had enslaved them both; and loud bursts of popular applause often greeted the successor of the Conqueror as he denounced the Anglican tyranny, and promised with the concurrence and support of the nation a speedy deliverance from its yoke. But strong in their legal rights, and their conspiracy with the foreigner, the territorial aristocracy and the Church contemned the democracy and their aspirations, and ridiculed the uncouth language of their addresses: whilst they regarded the King—Fitz Alan though he was—as a traitor to the conquering Norman caste of which he was the lawful head; and his appeals for support to their late democratic conquerors, as the lowest degradation of royal authority.

Encouraged by the popular demonstrations of loyalty to his government and person which his prolonged progress had everywhere evoked, King James took the desperate and fatal resolution of forcing the Norman caste and their creatures, the Corporation cliques, to return such members to Parliament as would be ready and willing to second his clement efforts for the civil and religious emancipation of his people from their yoke, emphatically declaring that he would have the odious Test and Penal Laws repealed, and that he would tolerate no man in any place of authority who was not prepared to carry out his views. This resolution he publicly declared in Council, at Whitehall, on Sunday, December the 11th, and afterwards issued a royal proclamation in the following terms: " His Majesty having by his gracious Declaration of the 4th day of April last granted a liberty of Conscience to all his subjects, and resolving not only to maintain the same, but to use his utmost endeavours that it may pass into a law and become an established security to after ages; hath thought fit to review the lists of the Deputy-Lieutenants and justices of the peace in the several counties, that those may be continued, who shall be ready to contribute what in them lies towards the accomplishment of so good and necessary a work; and such others added to them, from whom His Majesty may reasonably expect the like concurrence and assistance." The Lord-Lieutenants, summoned to the King's presence, were accordingly directed to appoint in their respective counties a commission composed of three noblemen who were empowered to influence the impending elections by visiting every influential elector and soliciting his vote in favour of candidates pledged to support the clement and patriotic policy of the King. But more than a half of them peremptorily refused; many others evaded their instructions by affecting to misunderstand them; and in the counties where the inquisition was made the resistance of the privileged classes was universal. All thought of an immediate convocation of Parliament had to be abandoned, but the baffled King would not give way. The hereditary successor of the very monarch who had bestowed on the Norman ancestors of this aristocracy and Church their honours and estates, and by his strength of will had forced them to the Norman Conquest, King

James scorned to be the mere head of their vast conspiracy against the nation, which exacted from him a constant and ferocious persecution of his subjects, and the ultimate adoption of a murderous and suicidal foreign policy. Misrepresented and maligned he blindly and madly strove to force them to break those legal chains, which, whilst stifling Puritan and democratic England, galled and constrained himself. Hitherto he had struck down individual members of the Norman caste, and at intervals Ormonde and Danby, Devonshire and Halifax, Clarendon and Rochester, Lumley and Nottingham had felt the weight of his displeasure; but now they fell in masses. At one fell swoop a host of the greatest nobles—the Duke of Somerset, Viscounts Newport and Falconberg, the Earls of Oxford, Shrewsbury, Derby, Dorset, Rutland, Abergavenny, Pembroke, Abingdon, Bridgewater, Northampton, Scarsdale, Thanet, Gainsborough and many others were at once dismissed from their Lord-Lieutenancies. Their satellites, the landed gentry on the bench and in the militia, shared the same fate, and many of the corporations lost their charters. Indeed all lord-lieutenants, deputy-lieutenants, justices of the peace, officers of the militia, mayors, aldermen, and other officials who had not in formal terms complied with the wishes of the King were dismissed from their public employments, and their places were filled with Dissenters and some few Roman Catholics. But the English co-religionists of James who were thus installed in public offices were less numerous than the band of Dutch adventurers whom the Dutch Deliverer subsequently raised to place and power in England. In a word we may say that for the second time since the Norman Conquest the aristocracy and their parasites were swept almost *en masse* from the public service. But undismayed they close their ranks, and as one man defiantly confront the King cajoling and deluding the nation as to the true character of their conflict with the Court until such time as their Dutch ally is disposed to rescue and reinstate them. The King next attacked his clerical adversaries. Hitherto the revolt of the Church had been but partial, although His Majesty's attempt to throw open its universities and correct its monstrous abuses had aroused a general spirit of suspicion and resentment in the bosom of that third element of the Triple tyranny—one and indivisible in origin and essence—which affected to sanctify the rest. But on the 27th of April, 1688, James published his second Declaration of Liberty of Conscience, and rashly commanded that it should be read in all the churches, immediately after Divine service, on two successive Sundays. As might have been foreseen, the clergy, like their fast allies the squires and nobles, reverence and uphold the sanctity and majesty of the inhuman and vindictive laws, which made them the collective tyrants of the throne and nation, and, of course, defy the King. The rebellion of the Church was headed by the Primate and six of his suffragans, who waited on King James with a Protest, in which they declared that Parliament—the permanent citadel of the conquering caste, which they would never voluntarily surrender, and of which they were the absolute possessors until 1832—could alone alter the laws; and they therefore decline to publish the King's illegal, but most righteous Declaration, which anticipated by a century and a half the civil and religious emancipation of Catholics and Dissenters; indeed, we may say of the nation. Hemmed in on every side, and baffled by the legally victorious caste, the infuriated King—believing that the people, like himself, perceived and scorned the chicanery and mendacity of their common adversaries, who unblushingly pretended that the laws which they had framed expressly for fettering the unconquered but betrayed democracy had now become a necessary bulwark against Popery and arbitrary power—threw the bishops—as they refused to give bail, and eagerly courted a cheap crown of martyrdom—into the Tower. But during their trial an incident occurred which decided the fate of King James and the future destinies of England. Some months before, His Majesty had announced by royal proclamation the approaching accouchement of the Queen; and the aristocracy and Church—in collusion with the Prince of Orange—immediately insinuated that their monarch, who, according to their own confession, "was never worse than his word," meditated the foulest of impostures. They therefore demanded that the Princess Anne and the Protestant ladies of the Court should be allowed to obtain certain proofs of the actual condition of the Queen, which they cynically observed might be easily given to women. This infamous proposal was naturally rejected with the sovereign scorn it merited. But on the birth of the Prince of Wales, the

King's delicacy in thus screening the Queen from personal outrage was made use of as a pretext for accusing both of the unnatural villainy of foisting on the nation a suppositious heir to the throne. A few days after the Norman caste and Dutch Stadtholder had seen their hopes of a legitimate fulfilment of their ambitious projects thus entirely blasted, the bishops appeared at the bar of the King's Bench to take their trial for libel. At once the menaced orders rally round their spiritual confederates. More than sixty Peers, with many other persons of distinction, sit out the trial, and overawe and intimidate both the judges and the jury. And the multitude— behind whose backs· and in whose despite a knot of aristocratic traitors and revolutionists had that very day summoned into England a foreign army to maintain their tottering tyranny—applauded the acquittal of men who were subsequently driven from their sees by their Dutch Deliverer for refusing to recognize the logical consequences of their disloyalty. Sublimely ignorant of the foul conspiracy, of which, in common with the King, they were the destined victims, and wildly conceiving that all resistance of royal authority must tend to popular liberty, the democracy blindly spurned the alliance of their royal and solitary champion and protector, who would have snapped the fetters of the caste and saved them from the bloody foreign yoke which it was contemptuously preparing to impose upon them. Deluded London was *en fête.* And amidst the confused din of gun-firing and the jangling of bells, and in the lurid glare of bonfires, the besotted and roaring mob burnt before the very doors of Whitehall an effigy of the Pope, unconscious that that Holy Father, Innocent XI.—in pursuance of a common policy—was marching hand-in-hand with the Dutch Protestant Deliverer to dethrone King James.

As we have already seen, the interests of our privileged classes and the Prince of Orange were inseparably joined together; for James had persistently striven to destroy the legalized despotism of the former, and had scornfully rejected the selfish and ambitious foreign policy of the latter, indignantly refusing, as a patriotic English King, at the behest of the Dutch Stadtholder, and in defence of purely Papal, Dutch, and German interests, to plunge his subjects into the countless horrors of a mad and wanton war with France. Therefore his treacherous and mendacious son-in-law and nephew—in concert with his Catholic and Protestant allies—was conspiring with our privileged classes to dethrone the King, as the only obstacle to his vast design of using England as a blind and passive instrument for the gratification of his boundless ambition and insatiable passion for war.

And in obedience to the instructions of Van Dykvelt and Zulestein, his envoys and emissaries at the English Court, the Anglicans, take advantage of the popularity they had acquired by the trial of the bishops to make overtures to the Dissenters for a close alliance, pretending that the rival claims of the Prince of Orange and the Prince of Wales to the throne were simply a question of Protestantism without distinction of sect against Catholicism. They protested that James's zeal for the abolition of the Test and Penal Laws sprang, not as the King said, from " his great clemency and tenderness to his people ; " but, so ran their shibboleth, from his determination to establish Popery and arbitrary power in England. And should they remain steadfast to their Protestant convictions, and withstand the proselytizing zeal of the King, then the Anglicans, with their traditional audacity, unblushingly assured the Dissenters, would King James and his handful of English Catholics—whose authority had been contemptuously and openly defied by every noble, squire, and parson who conceived his monstrous privileges endangered by the Declaration of Indulgence—then would King James and his handful of English Catholics "destroy us both." And in order to devise the best means "to prevent their imminent ruin," the Anglicans sought secret conferences with the Dissenters, whom they earnestly entreated to reject the alliance of the King, to whom they attributed all the political chicanery of the Church of which he was a member, and they, they should have added, were the close allies, declaring that as a Romanist he was not bound to keep faith with heretics, but might resort to any subterfuge in order either to convert or exterminate them. And if the Dissenters would forego "the fair opportunity of revenge" which was now within their grasp, and, regarding as a delusive snare that freedom from religious persecution, and that political as well as religious enfranchisement which the King had granted to them in defiance of Anglicanism, would make common cause, in their hour of deserved peril, with the nobility, clergy, and gentry; instead of attempting to restore, under the auspices of the King, and the guidance of Penn, the political supremacy and glory of democratic Puritanism, then would their late persecutors magnanimously extend to them that legal toleration, which, it was pretended, had been hitherto denied to them, lest their fellow-victims the Catholics should have also profited thereby. The Anglicans further expressed contrition for the past persecutions of the Church, throwing the blame, however, of every act of political vengeance which they had wreaked on their late Dissenting conquerors since the Restoration—under the mask of religion—upon the Court, to which they dared declare, in the face of heaven, they had reluctantly submitted. Finally they most mendaciously protested—and each successive year for the following century and a half bore witness to their perjury—that they would be no longer separated from their Dissenting "brothers" by ancient and cruel laws, which they professed—in bold defiance of historic fact—had yet been in the main levelled against their Roman Catholic fellow-countrymen. Moreover, that accomplished orator, the Marquis of Halifax—the unsuspected mouthpiece of the Prince of Orange—published at that time a letter of advice to the Dissenters, wherein he insinuated with much artifice the two-fold caution: that the Court was to be suspected, and that it would be neither Christian-like nor prudent "to hazard the public safety"—the Anglican despotism he meant, which an alliance of the Puritans with the King would have endangered—"either by desire of ease or revenge." The noble Marquis also declared with an amusing loftiness of tone: "That all their former haughtiness towards the Dissenters was for ever extinguished, and that the spirit of Persecution was turned into a spirit of Peace, Charity and Condescension. That the Church of England was convinced of its error, in being severe to them; and all thinking men were come to a general agreement, no more to cut ourselves off from the Protestants abroad, but rather enlarge the foundations upon which we are to build our defences against the common enemy." "The common enemy" being that decayed potentate the Sovereign Pontiff, who spurning the mild and innocent advances of the English King, had, out of mortal fear and hate of Catholic France, thrown himself passionately into the arms of their self-styled Protestant Protector, whose coffers, it is said, the Holy Father filled with the timely loan, which subsequently let loose the Dutch invading force on England, for our deliverance from the Papal yoke. Deluded by these hollow promises and monstrous calumnies, the Dissenters, with incredible infatuation, or perhaps from sheer helplessness, "waited" in utter ignorance of all precise knowledge of the Anglicans' foul conspiracy with the foreigner, "in expectation of seeing the effect of the Marquis's declaration on behalf of the Church party." In other words, by rejecting —from a blind fear of the Church of Rome, and in complete ignorance of its policy—the alliance of the King, the Dissenters abandoned the political field, together with the control of their future destinies, into the hands of their hitherto remorseless adversaries, the nobility, clergy, and gentry, who resisted the repeal of the Test and Penal Laws, less from fear of the King than of the democracy, against whose resumption of sovereign power those legal barriers had been expressly raised, and of which the demolition in their judgment would naturally and inevitably have led to the restoration of the Commonwealth in England. In a word, the Dissenters, with marvellous credulity, relied, of course in vain, on the benevolence of their eternal persecutors and conquerors for that civil and religious liberty and equality which the King had granted to them as a natural right, and which was co-extensive with that enjoyed by their posterity to-day. Thus King James, by his Declaration of Liberty of Conscience, lost the support of the nobility, clergy, and gentry, without winning to his side any section of the deluded democracy, who, destitute of leaders and organization, and cowed by a persistent and ferocious persecution of seventy and twenty years' duration, were, perhaps, incapable of affording any solid support to the throne.

We have already seen with what unnatural perfidy the Prince of Orange had conspired with the aristocracy and Church against both of his uncles, striving by the vilest means at once to force on Charles his miserable foreign policy, and to strip the Duke of York of his inheritance. And on the accession of James II., and while professing in common with the Princess the greatest affection for his father-in-law, he secretly abetted the ambitious designs of Monmouth—to thwart whose pretensions to the throne, which Shaftesbury warmly advocated, he had, through Halifax, in the preceding reign, quashed the Exclusion Bill—and though they both aimed at the same object, he suffered the Duke, in spite of the protests of the English Court, to equip an armament in Holland, and to form the plan of an invasion, in hopes of kindling civil war in England, and of facilitating his own seizure of the throne, by ruining at once a formidable rival and embarrassing and discrediting the King. It is even said that the Prince kept up a correspondence with the Duke, through his favourites, during the early stages of his enterprise, although Monmouth had, in his Manifesto, accused King James of being the author of the Fire of London and the Popish Plot; denounced him as an assassin, tyrant, and usurper; branded him as the murderer of King Charles, and vowed to avenge his reputed father's death in the blood of the royal fratricide. But when he heard Monmouth began to gather strength, and was proclaimed King, he not only hurried over the English regiments which were in the service of the States, but he likewise despatched his favourite Bentinck, as envoy extraordinary, to acquaint the King, "That though he looked upon the Duke of Monmouth to be a man of no great parts, yet he had a warlike genius, and was better skilled in the military art than any the King was to employ against him, and, therefore, if His Majesty pleased, he would not only lend him his troops, but come in person to head his army." The same proposal had been previously communicated to Skelton, the English ambassador at the Hague, who had transmitted it to the King, together with his suspicions of the sinister designs of the Prince. And James, believing that his son-in-law was capable of usurping his throne, after he had defeated Monmouth, dismissed the discredited Bentinck, telling him: "He should acquaint his master that their common interest did require the Prince's staying in Holland," and added: "He did not take His Highness's zeal for his service to be at that time seasonable." Moreover, the Prince subsequently received with open arms, and honoured with high command, the abandoned ruffian Kirke, who played the most villainous part in this rebellion, which Marlborough and Lumley had suppressed. Yet now they all—Prince, aristocracy, and Church—cast the whole odium of its merciless suppression on James alone. And having—on the birth of the Prince of Wales—painted the King "as black as hell," they proceed forthwith to dethrone him. The trial of the Bishops had been regarded as a crisis in the struggle between the Court and caste which would be decisive in its consequences, and their acquittal had left the baffled monarch apparently powerless and isolated. Yet the caste, conscious that no mendacity or slander could indefinitely postpone the ultimate coalition of the King and people for their political repression, had on the eve of their great victory, officially deputed—in obedience to a signal of the Prince of Orange—seven of their number to despatch a formal invitation to their Dutch Protector to invade England with a foreign army. We know not the precise terms of the momentous document which Devonshire, Danby, Shrewsbury, Lumley, Compton Bishop of London, Edward Russell, and Henry Sidney—all cursed with private grievances which prompted their dark deeds—signed and sent, in the name of the aristocracy and Church, to the Dutch Pretender; but practically those parricides and traitors said: "The birth of the Prince of Wales perpetuates our hopeless conflict with the Court, and supplants you as the King's presumptive heir. Therefore, in defence of our common cause, which his legitimacy ruins, we brand the child as counterfeit, and call on you to come and be our king, protesting that—in order to remain the tyrants of the nation which the Test and Penal Laws have made us—we will, on your appearance, at the head of a sufficiently powerful foreign force to ensure our personal safety, betray into your hands our native Court and country."

The Prince of Orange—whose wife's right of succession to the throne, which she had solemnly transferred to him, had been superseded by the birth of the Prince of Wales—realized all the importance of the supreme crisis. "It is now or never!" he exclaimed, as secretly and rapidly he collected troops and transports for a descent on England. The ties of blood, political honour, legitimate right, all were sacrificed to his ruling passion, an inextinguishable hate of France—the natural outcome of an insatiable ambition, which aimed at a virtual dictatorship of Europe—to gratify which, by enrolling England among her enemies, he now compasses the ruin of his uncle and father-in-law, and the usurpation of his throne. All Catholic as well as Protestant Europe—outside the menaced frontiers of fair France—support the unprincipled invader, for the patriotic refusal of King James to join the continental onslaught on the French had made the mighty league of Augsburg his implacable foe. So Austria, Holland, Spain, the German, Scandinavian, and Italian States, together with the Papacy itself, had formed, with the Prince of Orange and the English aristocracy and Church, a vast conspiracy for the dethronement of King James as the only obstacle to their grand design of making England their cheap and chief defence against the dreaded power of France. Surrounded with traitors—indeed the States-General of Holland, in justification of their share in the invasion, declared in a public manifesto to the European powers that the whole body of the nobility, clergy, and gentry had invited the Prince of Orange to undertake this enterprise—surrounded with traitors, the infatuated James was lulled in a blind security by the reiterated professions of devotion of the Prince and Princess of Orange. It was officially declared to the King: " That their Highnesses ever had, and were resolved ever to preserve a profound submission to His

Majesty as they thought themselves in duty bound by the laws of God and nature." And, "I am sure of my beloved daughter" is James's eternal answer to Louis's warnings of domestic treason and foreign levy, and his urgent offers of a powerful fleet and army for his succour and protection. And on the advice of those arch-traitors, Sunderland and Churchill, the betrayed King publicly and indignantly repudiated the alliance of France, and thus temporarily alienated and disgusted his solitary ally at the very moment when the Grand Monarque, by massing French troops on the Dutch frontier, and by proclaiming that any attack on the English King would be a declaration of war against himself, had practically baffled the designs on England of the Dutch Prince and people, and had filled them with a terror of French invasion. But the King's fond delusions were rudely dissipated by the publication of a forged memorial purporting to be an address from the Protestants of England and Scotland to the States of Holland, enumerating their grievances, and calling on the Prince of Orange to come over and redress, together with the Prince's reply thereto in the shape of Declarations addressed respectively to both countries. In these manifestoes this Dutch champion of the legalized despotism of the aristocracy, the Church, and their parasites and dependents, the Corporation cliques solemnly declared that King James's "setting up an illegal Commission for ecclesiastical affairs by which not only the Bishop of London was suspended, but the president and fellows of Magdalene College were arbitrarily turned out of their freeholds: His turning out of public employments all such as would not concur with His Majesty in the repeal of the Test and Penal Laws: His invading the privileges and seizing on the charters of most corporations, and placing Popish magistrates in some of them," and his imprisonment and trial of the seven bishops, had "made all men apprehend the loss of their lives, liberties, honours, and estates." And after accusing him of entertaining the preposterous design of enslaving the nation by means of an army of Irish Papists, proceeds to blacken the character of both the King and Queen by perhaps the most wanton and infamous aspersions recorded in history. He unblushingly asserts —and thus reveals the real motive of his enterprise—" That there were great and violent presumptions inducing His Highness to believe that the King's evil counsellors, in order to the gaining of more time for the effecting of their ill-designs, had published That the Queen had brought forth a son, though there had appeared, both during the Queen's pretended bigness and in the manner wherein the birth was managed, so many just and visible grounds of suspicion, that not only He Himself, but all the good subjects of the Kingdom did vehemently suspect That the pretended Prince of Wales was not born of the Queen. And though many both doubted of the Queen's bigness and of the birth of the child; yet there was not any one thing done to satisfy them or put an end to their doubts. That since his consort the Princess, and likewise he himself, had so great an interest in this matter, and such a right as all the world knew, to the succession of the crown," he thought it his duty, on private as well as public grounds, to appear in arms in England, not with any view to conquest, but only to defend himself "from the violence of these evil counsellors" in the prosecution of his benevolent enterprise. And in conclusion he said: "We have thought fit to declare that we will refer all," including "the inquiry into the birth of the pretended Prince of Wales," to a "lawful Parliament," knowing full well that all Parliaments were elected by and composed of the Conquering caste who—assailed by their legitimate King whose power they had eclipsed and whose alliance with the enslaved democracy they feared—were already pledged to hail him as their " great and glorious Deliverer."

His German allies having provided an army of 30,000 men for the defence of Holland during his absence, and the States-General, or, as some assert, his close ally Pope Innocent XI. having, to the great astonishment of the English and French ambassadors, advanced a loan of four million florins to defray the expenses of his expedition, the Prince of Orange fixed on the 5th or 6th of October as the day of embarkation. But, detained for more than a week by tempestuous weather, and beaten back by a furious storm on first venturing to sea, it was not until the 1st of November that he finally set sail from Helvoetsluys, and on the 5th his fleet of 50 men-of-war and 600 transports, having luckily eluded the more powerful armament of England under Lord Dartmouth, cast anchor in Torbay. On the following day his motley force of 15,000 men, bearing aloft the Dutch flag emblazoned with the specious but false device, "I will maintain the Protestant religion and the Liberties of England," advanced slowly through the rain and mire into the interior and in four days reached Exeter. The Prince had expected that on his first landing all the nobility and gentry of the West would have joined him, but, notwithstanding their universal disaffection, nine days passed without anything happening to encourage him; not a person of distinction had dared to come in. Moreover he perceived that the Mayor and Aldermen of Exeter visited him from fear rather than affection, and that he was badly in want of recruits, and still more of money, and therefore he began to despair of the success of his expedition. His troops, composed of men literally drawn from every country between the Gulf of Bothnia and the Bay of Biscay, were also discouraged; he himself thought of abandoning his enterprise, and in a council of war deliberated on a proposal to return to Holland. In his disappointment and dismay he publicly declared that he was betrayed, and vowed that he would re-embark and, in his turn, betray his accomplices, by transmitting to King James the secret correspondence of his subjects, so that his uncle might know where to strike. But one Burrington, a gentleman of Crediton, having set the evil example of open treason by joining his standard, the nobles and squires of Somerset, Devon, and Dorset flocked into Exeter in considerable numbers. The Prince, on the 15th of November, received them in a body, and made to the parricides and traitors the following hypocritical and canting speech. We may say here that on the eve of his embarkation for England, he had declared to the States-General of Holland that the "only aim of his expedition was the welfare of their country," and that "should he attain his ends he would set the States at greater liberty, and free them from the fear of their neighbours, and the haughty tyranny of those that would enslave them." And subsequently, when referring to the strongly expressed wish of the nobility that he would not risk his life by going in person to Ireland to fight King James, he described his and their Glorious Revolution in words of flame which cast a lurid glare upon two hundred thousand English corpses weltering in their gore, the unhappy victims of his baleful and blundering butcheries in Flanders. "They are only afraid," he writes to his Dutch favourite, Bentinck, "they are only afraid I shall get killed before I have done their work for them; as to their friendship, you know very well what that is worth in this country." But now he speaks in quite another strain. "Though we know not," says he to them in broken English, "though we know not all you persons, yet we have a catalogue of your names, and remember the character of your worth and interest in your country. You see, we are come according to your Invitation and our Promise. Our duty to God obliges us to protect the Protestant religion, and our love to mankind, your liberties and properties. We expected, you that dwelt so near the place of our landing, would have joined us sooner; not that it is now too late, nor that we want your military assistance so much as your countenance and presence, to justify our declared pretensions, rather than to accomplish our good and glorious designs. Though we have brought both a good fleet and a good army—to render these kingdoms happy, by rescuing all Protestants from Popery and Slavery, and Arbitrary Power, by restoring them to their rights and properties established by law, and by promoting of peace and trade, which is the soul of government, and the very life and blood of a nation—yet we rely more on the goodness of God and the justice of our cause than on any human force and power whatsoever. Yet, since God is pleased we shall make use of human means, and not expect miracles for our preservation and happiness; Let us not neglect making use of this glorious opportunity, but with prudence and courage put in execution our so-honourable purposes. Therefore, Gentlemen, Friends, and Fellow Protestants, We bid you and all your followers most heartily welcome to our Court and Camp. Let the whole world now judge if our pretensions are not just, generous, sincere, and above all price, since we might have even a Bridge of Gold to return back. But it is our Principle and Resolution, rather to die in a good cause than live in a bad one, well knowing that virtue and true honour is its own reward, and the happiness of mankind our great and only design."

Then the Prince of Orange—who exacted both the crown of England and the blood and treasure of its people as his recompense for maintaining with foreign bayonets the legalized system of caste despotism which King

James had vainly striven to subvert—then the Prince of Orange, I say, and the noblemen and gentlemen who were with him at Exeter, entered into an association or alliance for the better prosecution of their purely personal revolutionary projects, and to confuse, mislead, and paralyze the democracy, whose lasting servitude they planned under the mask of zeal for the Protestant religion and popular liberty—these parricides and traitors, the close allies of the Pope and the Catholic powers, promulgated from the camp of the Dutch army of invasion the following most audacious Declaration: "We do engage to Almighty God, and to His Highness the Prince of Orange, and with one another to stick firm to this cause, and to one another, in the defence of it, until our religion, laws, and liberties are so far secured to us in a Free Parliament, that they shall be no more in danger of falling under Popery and slavery. And whereas we are engaged in the common cause under the protection of the Prince of Orange, by which means his person is exposed to danger, and to the desperate and cursed designs of Papists and other bloody men; We do therefore solemnly engage to God, and to one another, That if any such attempts be made, we will pursue not only those that made it, but all their adherents, and all we find in arms against us, with the utmost severity of just revenge, to their ruin and destruction. And that the executing of any such attempt (which God, in His infinite mercy, forbid) shall not deprive us from pursuing this cause which we do now undertake, but it shall encourage us to carry it on with all the vigour that so barbarous an attempt shall deserve." Everywhere the descendants of our Norman conquerors turned traitors to the legitimate successor of the Norman Duke, who, on the battlefield of Hastings, gave to their ancestors absolute possession of both the soil and sovereignty of England. The Earl of Bath surrendered Plymouth to the Dutch Invader. Lord Delamere headed a rising of the nobles and squires of Cheshire, and took possession of Manchester on his way south. Danby raised the standard of revolt at York, and, with the peers and gentry of the North, effected a junction at Nottingham with the great lords of the Midland and Eastern counties, whom Devonshire and Chesterfield had summoned to arms. Lord Lumley seized Newcastle; Lord Shrewsbury occupied Bristol; Lord Herbert of Cherbury was in arms in Worcestershire; and the Duke of Norfolk, riding at the head of three hundred gentlemen into Norwich, declared for the Dutch Stadtholder.

The army, officered, as at all times, exclusively by the caste, was naturally the centre of a vast conspiracy against the King. Already Lords Colchester and Abingdon, with many other officers of distinction, had deserted to the enemy, and Lord Cornbury, the eldest son of the Earl of Clarendon, the King's brother-in-law, had by treachery partially succeeded in carrying over three regiments of cavalry to the Dutch camp. When James arrived at the head quarters of his army, numbering forty thousand men, at Salisbury, most of the principal officers waited on Lord Feversham, the commander-in-chief, and desired him to acquaint His Majesty "that upon any occasion they would be ready to spill the last drop of their blood in his service, yet they could not in conscience fight against a Prince who was come over with no other design than to procure the calling of a free parliament for the security of their religion and liberties." The appearance of our last English King in the midst of an English army was the signal for the blackest episode of this most infamous revolution. A foul conspiracy was formed by the arch-traitor Churchill, the ruffian Kirke, and Trelawny, a brother of one of the imprisoned bishops, to arrest the King and carry him off to the invaders' camp. And to facilitate the execution of this odious project, these parricides and would-be regicides urged their royal master to visit the outpost at Warminster, in order to inspect Kirke's division. The unsuspecting King consented, and Kirke and Trelawny hastened to rejoin their forces on the pretence of making preparations for the royal reception and review. A sudden indisposition of the King alone prevented the perpetration of this supreme act of treachery and treason, and the baffled traitors, with Churchill's brother, Berkeley, and the Duke of Grafton, fled by night to the enemy's quarters at Axminster. Strengthened by the adhesion of the ruling caste, the Dutch Invaders steadily advanced on Salisbury, whilst the English army, disorganized and demoralized by the universal disaffection or desertion of its officers, commenced a disorderly retreat. The first stage of their retrograde movement was Andover, where Prince George of Denmark and the Duke of Ormond, after supping with the King, took horse, and rode off with Lord Drumlanrig and other officers of rank and quality to the enemy's camp. Surrounded by traitors, capable at any moment of reviving Churchill's horrid plot, King James now lost heart and fled to London, followed by the wreck of his betrayed but unconquered soldiery, who finally took up their quarters in the suburbs of the capital.

The King reached Whitehall to learn that his favourite daughter Anne, together with her favourite, Lady Churchill, and Compton, Bishop of London, had left that very day to join the rebel lords at Nottingham. "God help me," was the piteous cry of our modern Lear, bursting into tears, "God help me! My own children have forsaken me." Yet he summoned a council of some forty or fifty peers and prelates then in town—who, far from their Dutch protector, again swore fealty to him—and despatched commissioners to Hungerford to treat with their ally his son-in-law. But these were his last acts of royal power. The council soon dispersed, and several of its members—including the Earls of Clarendon and Oxford and the Duke of Somerset—went over to the enemy. Indeed, the tide of aristocratic treason and defection flowed steadily and placidly westward. Every day the Court and camp of

England dwindled to complete extinction, to revive in the Court and camp of the Dutch invader. The situation of the King was now quite desperate, and the Prince of Orange, while affecting a willingness to treat, resorted to a system of veiled intimidation to force James to take flight. He declined, at least, a public conference, with Lords Halifax, Nottingham, and Godolphin—masked traitors all—whom James had sent to Hungerford as his commissioners; and he deputed the Earl of Clarendon—who had publicly and grossly insulted the King in his misfortunes—and the Earl of Oxford to treat with them. Through these parricides and traitors he practically demanded an instantaneous share of James's throne; and though he verbally consented, on the conditions of a conqueror, to a temporary suspension of hostilities, yet he never slackened for a moment the rapid march of his troops on the capital. Moreover, the deluded mob—a favourite weapon of the Prince of Orange, both in England and in Holland—was again incited to attack the King and his co-religionists. A proclamation published in the Prince's name—but afterwards disowned by him—commanded everyone to search out, seize, and treat as bandits all Catholics who, contrary to law, were in possession of defensive weapons, for (so ran that atrocious manifesto) a certain king, in league with the King of France, had sworn to extirpate the Protestant faith, and unless the Papists were at once secured they would destroy by fire and massacre both London and its citizens. This incident roused the fury of the people against the King and Catholics almost to madness, and an inflammatory but senseless doggerel, called "Lillibullero"—which gave expression to another insane charge the Prince of Orange brought against King James of designing to enslave and Romanize England by means of an army of Irish Papists—kept alive the popular frenzy and delusion, and blinded the nation, until too late, as to the real and lasting usurpation and tyranny which the Dutch prince and the conquering Norman caste were then consolidating, by foreign force and foulest fraud, without their intervention, in their midst. Thus did his foreign and domestic enemies, resorting to the odious tactics of the Popish Plot, again, by terror of the deluded mob, hasten King James's flight.

Bereft of reason by the awful treachery and desertion of which he was the helpless victim, the King gives way to the dictates of despair. He sends the Queen—who shares his terrors, for she had also been subjected to intimidation and assured that she, in common with her predecessors, was liable to Parliamentary impeachment—and the Prince of Wales to France under the escort of the celebrated Count of Lauzun, then in exile here. Lauzun's whole career had been a series of romantic escapades, and his character is best illustrated by his promise to this same Queen on his departure for the Boyne campaign "to bring the usurping Prince of Orange a captive and in chains to her feet." They escape, under his conduct, from Whitehall, by the backstairs, to the waterside, and cross the Thames in an open boat, on a dark, tempestuous night. Queen Mary—a chaste and beautiful princess of the house of Este, with her child, the infant Prince of Wales, in his nurse's arms—waits under the walls of Lambeth Church, exposed to the pitiless fury of the winter's blast and the pelting rain, while a coach was got ready at a neighbouring inn. This shameful scene of the betrayal and abandonment of the Conqueror's infant heir by the descendants of his Norman followers was the grave of their boasted loyalty and honour, and should be emblazoned on their every escutcheon as a brand of indelible infamy. Followed on horseback by a friend of Lauzun, they pass unobserved through Greenwich, and reaching Gravesend in safety, embark in the yacht that lay ready to receive them. In a few hours they landed at Calais. The next night the King—after leaving orders to Lord Feversham to disband his forces as incapable of offering "resistance to a foreign army and a poisoned nation"—escaped from his palace, and with but two attendants made his way to Sheerness and went on board a hoy in the offing, bound for France.

This sudden dissolution of all government was the signal for the wildest anarchy and confusion. During the 11th and 12th of December London was in the hands of a riotous mob, and that period of terror and outrage was followed by what was long remembered as the "Irish night," a scene of strange and grotesque horror which is happily unique in our history. The Prince of Orange, or his partisans, in order to throw the nation into a state of universal tumult and trepidation, and so prepare the popular mind for his reception as a saviour of society, had recourse to an effectual but infamous stratagem. A party of his emissaries, having the dress and air of country fellows, arrive about midnight at Westminster and cause a sudden uproar and panic by reporting that the Irish Papists whom Feversham had disbanded were again in arms, and had reached Uxbridge in full march on London, putting all before them to fire and sword. Within an hour the dreadful rumour filled the doomed city. The alarm-bells were rung, the drums of the train-bands sounded the reveille, the affrighted citizens, roused from their first slumber, stood to their weapons; lights blazed in every window. In their distraction and terror the Londoners fancied they saw in the distance the smoke of the conflagrations which announced the approach of the Irish Papists and heard the dying groans of the Protestant victims of Irish savagery. And so complete had been the measures taken by the authors of this nefarious plot that a general terror spread itself that very night over the whole kingdom. Every important city and town—alarmed by identic letters, framed to delude and terrify the ignorant, and delivered all at once—presented the same strange and humiliating spectacle of armed multitudes awaiting the approach of Papistical hordes, who, they had been warned, were bent on an indiscriminate slaughter of the Protestants, attended with all the unspeakable horrors of the atrocious Irish massacre of 1641. But when day dawned the nation—scared by a phantom army, yet ignoring the presence of the Dutch—was sobered by the humiliating conviction that it had been the dupe of a foul and malignant trick, attributed by some to the Prince of Orange himself, but more commonly ascribed by the popular opinion of the time to Marshal Schomberg, his lieutenant. It learned with shame that the Irish troops whom James had so unadvisedly brought into England, and whose presence was so prejudicial to his cause, did not number three thousand men.

Meanwhile the Dutch army had advanced to Windsor, where the Prince of Orange and his English adherents were thrown into the wildest confusion by the startling intelligence that King James had been detained at the moment of his departure. The hoy on which he had embarked had been run ashore near Sheerness for ballast, and about eleven o'clock at night, before the tide could float her, had been boarded by fishermen in search of fugitives. The appearance of the King, disguised as a country gentleman, at once attracted their attention. "This is Father Petre," shouted one fellow; "I know him by his hatchet face." And swearing that their prisoner should not depart until he had been examined by a magistrate, they immediately seize and search the King, and finally carry him ashore at Feversham. There, at an obscure inn, amidst the insults of the deluded rabble who took him for a Jesuit— that incarnation of the Evil One, the Anglicans to ruin James had taught them to believe—the unhappy monarch declares himself their King. For very shame of these indignities, which by their treason they had brought upon King James, the peers and prelates—who had already sent a pressing invitation to the Dutch invader to hasten to the capital and fill the vacant throne—despatched Lord Feversham with two hundred Life Guards to protect the King from insult, but to allow him full liberty of action, and to encourage and facilitate his further flight. But James no longer desired to escape. Lords Middleton and Winchelsea had pointed out to him that his throne would have been for ever lost had he vacated it by flight; but by remaining he was King, and might challenge his right: and the Dutch prince could not now dethrone him without playing the odious part of an usurper, and casting on himself and wife the indelible stain of filial baseness and ingratitude. James's broken spirit revived at these suggestions, and he resolved to return to his capital. On the other hand the Prince of Orange—believing the King had gone—had already assumed the attributes of sovereignty, and his principal adherents had arranged among themselves the different offices of state they were to fill; but when undeceived, they, in this supreme crisis of their fortunes, at once resorted to the very plan which the merest accident alone had thwarted. As we have already seen, they were stealthily effecting, with a foreign army, a revolution from which the people were jealously excluded, with a single eye to their own interest and ambition, under the fraudulent and hypocritical pretext, that the King and Queen, in order to gain time to establish Popery and arbitrary power in England by means either of armed bands of Irish Papists or of the military power of France, had been guilty of the unnatural villainy of foisting on the nation a suppositious heir to the throne. They therefore feared delay, which would have unmasked their fraud, and might have brought about a coalition of the King and nation—their common victims—for their own destruction. And to prevent this possible catastrophe they now resolve to frighten the infatuated James to a repetition of his insane attempt to escape out of his kingdom. His messenger, Lord Feversham—whom he had sent from Rochester with a letter to the Prince inviting him to St. James's with what number of troops he might think fit, to confer with the King on the affairs of the nation—was placed under arrest for disbanding the English army which had remained loyal in spite of the treason and desertion of its officers; and Zulestein—soon to be created Earl of Rochford—was despatched by William to decline a conference, and to forbid James to approach the capital. But the Dutchman missed him by the way, and the King entered London in triumph amidst the loudest acclamations of joy of all classes of the citizens, the ringing of bells, the burning of bonfires, together, says a contemporary writer, "with every other proof that the people who hated Popery loved the King." It is evident that the presence of the foreign invader—which was as great a surprise to the nation as to the King himself, and as gross an outrage to the national as to the royal susceptibilities—had revived his waning popularity; and that the people now began to perceive that they had been "poisoned" against their solitary protector the King, by the slanders and mendacities of the aristocracy and Church, whose legalized despotism he had vainly striven to subvert, and of a Prince whose murderous and ambitious foreign policy, he, with the truest patriotism, had steadily rejected, and whose pretensions to the English throne he had blasted by the birth of the Prince of Wales.

But his enemies, perceiving their danger, would allow him no respite. They immediately resolved on a desperate venture which should make or mar their fortunes. Scarcely had James re-entered his Palace when Zulestein delivered his insolent message. And soon afterwards the King was filled with fresh terrors by the announcement of Feversham's imprisonment. Yet on the following day he sent the Earl of Musgrave with his compliments to the Prince of Orange, who had by this time reached Sion House, while the Dutch guards had occupied Kensington and Chelsea. There at nightfall they received orders to take military possession of the Palaces of Whitehall and St. James's either by fair means or open force. St. James's was entered at ten o'clock, and a little later a detachment of horse and foot, under the command of Count Solmes, marched rapidly through the Park to Whitehall, and took up a position in order of battle opposite the Coldstream Guards, who were on duty at the Palace. As the English seemed indisposed to dislodge, the Dutch marched up to them with their matches lighted, as if about to commence an attack. The Earl of Craven—a distinguished veteran of eighty—who commanded the Coldstream Guards, declared that no foreign prince should make a King of England a prisoner in his own palace so long as he retained life. And one well-directed volley from the Coldstream muskets might yet have stung the outraged and deluded nation to prompt and decisive intervention in its own affairs. I do not doubt that the rattle of a Dutch fusilade through the corridors of Whitehall and the groans of the dying would have opened all eyes to the true character of an enterprise, which, under the mask of all the virtues, violated every principle and tie the world holds sacred; and that it would inevitably have rallied round the Stuarts' Throne, the oppressed democracy, of which it was the solitary and vanishing defence, against combined aristocratic and foreign tyranny, usurpation and conquest. But James, who was retiring to rest, having vainly desired Count Solmes to leave him in charge of his own people for that night, forbade all resistance, and, at his command, the Coldstream Guards sullenly abandoned their posts. By eleven o'clock at night the Dutch were in full possession of the palace, and double guards were placed over the person of the King. Thus, by a singular irony of fate, was our last King of English blood made a prisoner in his own capital, amidst its slumbering citizens, by the Dutch guards of that very prince whose conquered countrymen, at the command of Cromwell, had, by the Perpetual Edict, excluded not simply from the stadtholderate of his own country, but from its military and naval services.

The King again retired to bed and to sleep, but about one o'clock in the morning he was roused from his first slumber by a deputation of noblemen, who came with a message from the Prince of Orange, and insisted on an immediate audience. Admitted to his bedside, they delivered to him the following order from his son-in-law and nephew :—" We desire you, the Lord Marquis of Halifax, the Earl of Shrewsbury, and the Lord Delamere, to tell the King that it is thought convenient, for the great quiet of the city, and the great safety of his person, that he do remove to Ham, where he shall be attended by his guards, who will be ready to preserve him from any disturbance." Having read this extraordinary command, he said he would comply with it. Whereupon the lords desired him to leave early, before ten o'clock that very morning, so as to avoid meeting the Prince on his way to London, where he would be in a few hours. The King again acquiesced, and the lords took their leave; but when they had reached the privy chamber they were recalled, and told by the King that "he had forgot to acquaint them with his resolutions before the message came, to send my Lord Godolphin next morning to the Prince, to propose his going back to Rochester; he finding by the message Monsieur Zulestein was charged with that the Prince had no mind that he should be at London, and therefore he now desired that he might rather return to Rochester than go to any other place." The lords blandly replied that they had no authority to accede to His Majesty's request, but that they would immediately acquaint the Prince therewith, not doubting but that his answer would be to His Majesty's satisfaction. A message was accordingly despatched in hot haste to His Highness, who was still at Sion House, and who, delighted at the success of his stratagem, ordered Mynheer Bentinck to write a letter, which reached Whitehall before daybreak, expressing his ready compliance with the King's proposal. The English commissioners of the Dutch invader, who were effecting and superintending the final overthrow of our ancient Norman Monarchy, lost no time in the execution of their momentous mission. The royal barge was immediately got ready and brought round to Whitehall stairs, where the King—with the acclamations of London still ringing in his ears—having taken leave of the Spanish ambassador and other persons there present, went on board, attended by two English and three Scotch lords. The Marquis of Halifax stood sullenly aloof, covering his monstrous treason by affected indignation at his bootless errand to Hungerford; but his brother traitors, the Earl of Shrewsbury and Lord Delamere, appeared much moved as they betrayed the legitimate successor of the Norman Conqueror—who held his Crown by the same title they held their honours and estates—into the hands of their allies the Dutch. In a storm of wind and rain the royal barge put off from land, and, surrounded by boats filled with Dutch soldiers, dropped slowly down the river. The angry billows of the noble stream buffeted furiously the frail bark, and seemed to protest against the folly and infatuation of its native Monarch by thus retarding his mad flight. Not until nine o'clock at night did he reach Gravesend, where he was met by some troops of Dutch cavalry, who, the next day, guarded him by land to Rochester.

The same day—the 18th of December—the Dutch invader marched into London—which was already occupied by his motley bands of foreign mercenaries—and about three o'clock in the afternoon came to St. James's. It rained very heavily, yet a great crowd had assembled to witness his arrival. But the Prince—probably resenting their enthusiastic reception of King James the day before—took the road through the park to the palace, and the disappointed and snubbed citizens, drenched to their skins, dispersed to their homes. This incident served to increase the indignation which the Prince's midnight arrest and subsequent unnatural intimidation of his uncle and father-in-law, in spite of his submission, had excited in the breasts of both the army and the people. They began to suspect, what was indeed self-evident, " that this specious undertaking would prove to be only a disguised and designed usurpation." But

"Sans berger que peut le troupeau."

The public bodies, however, waited upon him with a fulsome address, in which, referring to the rapid success of his enterprise, they said, " astounded we think it marvellous." They further assure him that " led by the hand of heaven," he had preserved " our laws, which are our ancient title to our lives, liberties, and estates, and without which, this world were a wilderness." The lords spiritual and temporal, about seventy in number, also repaired to St. James's to offer their congratulations, and, at his desire, adjourned to the House of Lords, to consider the most effectual measures for convoking a parliament for the regulation of the affairs of the nation, upon the basis of his Declaration, which he formally presented to them for that purpose. After reading that unique document, and voting him their thanks for his " so great kindness to these kingdoms," in coming over, they proceed : " And we do hereby declare that we will, with our utmost endeavours, assist His Highness in the obtaining of such a Parliament with all speed, wherein our laws, our liberties and properties, may be secured, and the Church of England in particular, with a due liberty to Protestant Dissenters, and, in general, the Protestant religion and interest over the whole world may be supported and encouraged, to the glory of God, the happiness of the established government in these kingdoms, and the advantage of all princes and States in Christendom, that may be herein concerned." In other words, the grateful peers and prelates eagerly and enthusiastically adopted their " great and glorious deliverer's " most insane foreign policy—which he had so persistently and vainly striven to impose upon Kings Charles and James—and in pursuance of it " supported and encouraged... the Protestant religion and interest over the whole world," by making England the stolid and quixotic champion and practical paymaster of Pope Innocent XI. of Rome himself, and of the

Catholic despots of Austria, Spain, Bavaria, and Savoy. Yet so insecure did the parricides and traitors feel, whilst James remained in the country, and might appeal to the nation for support, that the whole assembly signed, with four or five exceptions, the same engagement or association which the nobility and gentry had already subscribed at Exeter, pledging themselves to mutual support until the objects of their movement were accomplished. The next day the Duke of Norfolk, by whose influence the nobility and gentry of the eastern counties had been induced to declare for the Prince of Orange, was received by His Highness with the highest honours at the palace of St. James's.

The King soon hears of these proceedings, and is confirmed by them in his fatal resolution of escaping to France. His enemies afford him every facility; the snare is transparent even to his disturbed and shallow intellect. The garden of the house in which he lodged descended to the river, and was easily accessible to the boats of several vessels, which lay at no great distance, ready to set sail. Yet, although closely watched by Dutch soldiers on all other sides, the back door of the house was left without any guard. Fully conscious that there was nothing his rival so much desired, or his friends dreaded as his flight, he was yet constrained by that inexorable master, an abject and panic fear. Visions of death under every horrid aspect—the axe of the executioner, the poisoned cup, the assassin's dagger—haunted his heated and disordered imagination, and paralyzed every manly faculty. Nothing was lost had he been but true to himself. Two ways were yet open to him, either of which would have led him back to his throne. But resistance or submission is alike impossible to the betrayed craven. In vain does Dundee boldly urge an appeal to arms. "The question, sir," he exclaims, "the question, sir, is whether you shall stay in England or fly to France? Whether you shall trust to the returning zeal of your native subjects, or rely on a foreign power? Here you ought to stand, keep possession of a part, and the whole will submit by degrees. Resume the spirit of a king; summon your subjects to their allegiance; your army, though disbanded, is not annihilated; give me your commission, and I will collect ten thousand of your troops, I will carry your standard at their head through England, and drive before you the Dutch and their Prince." It is true that the King acknowledged the soundness and feasibility of Dundee's manly counsel, but said that it would lead to a civil war, and expressed his conviction that the nation would soon recover its senses without an appeal to that terrible ordeal. In vain does Lord Middleton, with his other friends, Aylesbury, Lichfield, Arran, and Dumbarton, counsel submission. Nothing, they assure him, in substance, if not in words, could prevent his regaining his throne, if he, the proud Norman heir of their creator the Conqueror, would publicly renounce what was portentously called the dispensing and suspending power; and—placing himself unreservedly at the head of the vast and permanent conspiracy which the nobility, clergy, and gentry had formed against the nation since their unexpected restoration to all power by the traitor Monk—would accept the *rôle* of a mere titular King of a revengeful and conquering caste. All of them unite in deprecating the suicidal act of flight, and in pointing out its natural and inevitable consequences a virtual abdication of the throne, which latter consummation, I suppose, few men in England desired beside the Prince of Orange and his immediate and implicated partisans. Lord Middleton, above all, implored James to remain, though in the remotest part of his dominions. "Your Majesty," said he, "may throw things into confusion by your departure, but it will be but the anarchy of a month; a new Government will soon be settled, and then you and your family are ruined for ever." But no remonstrance could revive a spark of courage in the breast of this unhappy victim of unnatural and unparalleled treachery and treason, whose very misfortunes predisposed him to become the facile subject of a ghastly and grotesque scare. The arrest of Feversham, the sudden seizure by Dutch Guards of the posts round Whitehall, and the visit an hour after midnight of the three traitor lords to the bedside of the King, ordering him to quit before midday the capital which had just welcomed his return with boundless enthusiasm, were three acts of a solemn farce, which the cowardice of James converted into a domestic and national tragedy. The miserable sham appeared to the eyes of its wretched victim in the light of a stern reality. King James believed, as was intended, that his son-in-law meditated his death by poison or assassination. And prompted by this craven fear, he resolves on immediate flight. But first he wrote a Declaration of his motives for this strange procedure. He declared that his life was in danger from the evil designs of a nephew, who, without a cause, had painted him as "black as hell," by accusing him of the unnatural villainy of foisting on the nation a suppositious heir to the throne, in order to rob his own daughter of her birthright; and who, on this foul aspersion, which he knew in his conscience was false, as well as on the flimsy pretext of defending the religion and liberties of England, had invaded his dominions, seized him at midnight in his own palace, and driven him from his capital. Therefore, to preserve his life and liberty of action, he withdrew only until the country opened its eyes to the false pretences by which it had been deluded, and summoned him to return. This Declaration of the King, like all his royal utterances, was literally true, and had he remained in England, the mendacities and slanders which hurled him from his throne must have been unmasked to the confusion and ruin of his enemies. It was infamously false to demonstration that James (*a*) made "all men apprehend the loss of their lives, liberties, honours, and estates;"

(*b*) that he foisted on the nation a supposititious heir to the throne; (*c*) or that he designed to establish Popery and arbitrary power either by means of an army of Irish or French Papists. But it is quite true that, prompted by his " great clemency and tenderness to his people," he staked and lost his crown in the mad, but magnanimous attempt to free them from the legalized tyranny of the aristocracy, who—freshly remembering their dismal overthrows at Newbury, Marston Moor, and Naseby, at Preston, Dunbar, and Worcester—still deemed their odious Test and Penal Laws as necessary barriers against the Revolution, without which the democracy might yet again, and finally, sweep away the Conqueror's Baronage, Church, and throne. But morally just as was his cause, our modern Lear, maddened by his misfortunes, fled from his prison-house on Sunday, the twenty-third of December, about three o'clock in the morning, without communicating his design even to Lord Dumbarton, who lay in his chamber, and who did not awake until after the King's departure. And, accompanied by his natural son, the Duke of Berwick, and two attendants, he repaired on horseback, through storm and darkness, to the place appointed at the river's side, where Captain MacDonnel, with a small skiff, waited to receive him. He was immediately conveyed on board a smack, which set sail with a favourable wind, and after a rapid voyage he landed on the shores of France; abandoning without a struggle a surprised and deluded, but loyal and generous people, who were inert only because of his inertness, as a prey to the conquering Norman caste, who had again with foreign force and foulest fraud subdued them and the sceptre of his ancestor, the Norman Duke, to the bloody sway of their Dutch Deliverer, and bearing with him the peaceful fortunes of England. For that very day the Prince of Orange, on receiving the joyful tidings of King James's flight, sent a peremptory order to the French ambassador to leave England within twenty-four hours, thus plunging this country—in prompt fulfilment of his promise to the Dutch States-General—into a disastrous war of nine years with the French, in defence of purely German, Dutch, and Papal interests, which was followed, after a four years' truce and in pursuance of the same Dutch policy, by the longer, costlier, and bloodier War of the Spanish Succession.

And thus was inaugurated a wanton and sanguinary system of foreign policy, unknown to our history under our legitimate kings, which squandered the blood and treasure of England, not in defence of English honour and interests, but for the gratification of the inflated ambition of our petty foreign rulers and the aggrandizement of their Continental States.

The legitimate and national monarchy having been thus destroyed, the lords spiritual and temporal desire the Prince to summon by circular letters a Convention Parliament, and in the meantime to take upon himself the administration of public affairs. But as the peers had manifested an intention of holding the Prince to the letter of his Declaration, he introduces a new element into the discussion by inviting all the gentlemen then in town who had sat in the House of Commons during the reign of Charles II., together with the principal members of the Corporation of London, to concur in this request. The Convention accordingly met to deliberate, in the words of the Prince, " under the shelter of my arms." And first these delegates of the aristocracy and Church, and of their parasites, the Corporation cliques

—under the protection of the Dutch army of invasion then in occupation of London—with marvellous audacity and plausibility, declare "that King James having endeavoured to subvert the Constitution of the kingdom by breaking the original contract between King and people, and by the advice of Jesuits and other wicked persons having violated the fundamental laws, and having withdrawn himself out of the kingdom, had abdicated the government, and that the throne had thereby become vacant."

But they omit to tell us that "the Constitution of the kingdom," as they phrase it, which King James had "endeavoured to subvert," was the Restoration despotism of the aristocracy and Church, and that "the fundamental laws" which he had "violated" were those modern "Bloody Statutes"—the Corporation Act, the Act of Uniformity, the Conventicle, Five Mile, Test, and Parliamentary Test Acts—on which the Cavalier Parliament had astutely founded that atrocious despotism. And having on the false pretence of dread and apprehension of their own ally, the Church of Rome, thus formally deposed King James and stripped the infant Prince of Wales of his right of succession to the throne, they proceed forthwith to dispose of the Stuarts' glorious heritage. As we have already seen, the Prince of Orange was pledged in honour to submit to the decisions of the Convention Parliament; and it is evident that many of its members shared the fond delusion of the Duchess of Marlborough, who said—speaking in defence of her husband and herself—"I do solemnly protest, that if there be truth in any mortal, I was so very simple a creature, that I never dreamt of his being King. I imagined that the Prince of Orange's sole design was to provide for the safety of his own country, by obliging King James to keep the laws of ours; and that he would go back as soon as he had made us all happy: that there was no sort of difficulty in the execution of this design; and that to do so much good would be a greater pleasure to him than to be the king of any country upon earth." But no sooner was it proposed by some to confer the crown solely on the Princess, and by others to establish a regency, than the Prince, seeing the great object of his ambition, for which he had conspired for sixteen years, about to slip for ever from his grasp, promptly and decisively intervenes. He summoned the principal peers, his co-conspirators, to his presence, and knowing, after all, that they could not possibly do without him, he did not seek to conciliate them, but bluntly told them that he would neither be regent nor accept a crown dependent on his wife, adding "He would not think of holding anything by apron-strings." But, if they chose to offer him the crown entirely to himself and for his whole life, he would freely accept it, and if not he would return to Holland, having done that which he had promised. The Convention Parliament was therefore obliged to reconsider its decisions and come to a different settlement. And, as some with reason feared the intervention of the nation, and others that the Prince would seize the crown, they, under the pressure of circumstances of their own creation, declared the Prince and Princess of Orange King and Queen of England, "And that the sole and full exercise of the royal power be only in, and executed by the said Prince of Orange." Then this Iago of politics, the victims of whose treachery were his nearest kindred, unblushingly declared: "This is certainly the greatest proof of the trust you have in me that can be given, which is the thing which makes us value it the more: And as I had no other intention in coming hither than to preserve your religion, laws and liberties, so you may be sure that I shall endeavour to support them." This was the Prince's public and official history of his share in the Glorious Revolution; his private and confidential narrative of the same event will bear repeating here, if only for the sake of contrast and comparison. Referring to the prayer of the aristocracy that he would not risk his life by fighting James in Ireland, he writes to his Dutch favourite Bentinck: "They are only afraid I shall get killed before I have done their work for them; as to their friendship, you know very well what that is worth in this country." Indeed, his declaration of loyalty to his makers was but a mere formality, for the aristocracy and Church were fully conscious that their monstrous privileges and properties could never be endangered either by their Dutch or German nominees and creatures, who as foreigners could never secure the national sympathies in opposition to themselves. Henceforth the great name and prestige of king was intentionally and indissolubly interlinked with the tyranny and usurpation of a caste, who, masters by right of conquest of that fountain of all their honours and estates, the Conqueror's throne itself, filled it at will with foreigners of their own selection. And, by an unwritten compact, the nominal Dutch or German head of this vast and permanent conspiracy against the nation was allowed to preoccupy the public mind with wanton and sterile continental warfare, whilst the aristocracy and Church enjoyed in perfect tranquillity that absolute possession of the soil which their Norman ancestors had conquered for them on the battle-field of Hastings, together with a complete control of the legislature and government of England.

This Glorious Revolution, as it was termed, not only gave a legal consecration and practically a right of reconquest to the old Norman domination, but it placed on the throne a prince who, owing his crown to the aristocracy, was but a puppet in their hands. This nominee of the lords was the head of the State Church. The revenue of this State Church was now virtually the property of the lords. This political and religious organization formed a common system, and it is this combination of spiritual and temporal interests, together with, until recently, the exclusive possession of the national universities, which has hitherto given to the Anglican Establishment, and the political system of which it is the spiritual offspring and representative, energy and durability. The Church now transferred its allegiance to an oligarchy presided over by a nominal and alien king. And this Dutch king, together with his German successors, was bound by coronation oaths to maintain to the utmost of his power the quasi-religious institution of which he had been made supreme temporal head, and "to preserve unto the bishops and clergy all such rights and privileges as by law do or shall appertain unto them, or any of them."

"Nothing," says Hallam in tones which happily belong to the past, "nothing was done by the multitude; no new men, either soldiers or demagogues, had their talents brought forward by this rapid and peaceful revolution." Indeed the English king and nation were the common and helpless victims of that infamous conspiracy of the aristocracy and Church with the Dutch prince and ruling caste, who had for sixteen years waged a dark and unnatural warfare against both Charles and James, of calumny and imposture, of fraud and intrigue, of mendacity and canting hypocrisy; and who, seeing their legitimate pretensions to the absolute sovereignty of the British Isles frustrated by the birth of the Prince of Wales, suddenly attained their ends by foreign force and the foulest domestic treachery and treason. That England which under the Commonwealth had seen vanquished Holland a suppliant at her feet, now beheld a Dutch army in possession of London, a Dutch prince seated on her throne, his Dutch followers—the Bentincks and Keppels, the Schombergs and Ginkells, the Auverquerques and Zulesteins—enrolled among her nobles; his Dutch generals at the head of motley bands of foreign mercenaries, interspersed with British troops, conquering and confiscating for her own masters her Sister Island; and she herself, passive and helpless, transformed into a political satellite of Holland by the grateful parricides and traitors whom the Prince of Orange had practically and consciously enthroned. And, booted and spurred, this bastard Alexander was lifted by our aristocracy and Church—traitors alike to their native king and country—into the saddle of the British Bucephalus, and in wanton quest of mere military glory that ever fled from him, the rank cosmopolite adventurer urged the hitherto invincible steed through the fire and smoke of eight inglorious campaigns, during which mad career of blundering disasters it staggered and fell beneath him from sheer exhaustion on the bloody fields of Steinkirk and Neerwinden. And having drained it of its best blood the inept and callous rider stigmatized as vile the war-horse which, pitted against far mightier antagonists, the traitor Marlborough guided with perfect ease to complete and endless victory.

Moreover, the aristocracy and Church perpetuated with foreign bayonets their infamous usurpation and tyranny by concluding a treaty with the States-General of Holland, which enabled them for the next two generations, in times of popular commotion, to pour Dutch troops into England for the maintenance of the extraordinary *régime* their own countrymen had established.*

* The most complete and utter condemnation of the Glorious Revolution is the subsequent high treason of the aristocratic revolutionists against their Dutch Deliverer himself, whom they would have replaced by King James had the latter consented to condone the surpassing treachery of every parricide and traitor.

x

VI.

DESPOTISM OF THE NOBILITY, CLERGY, AND GENTRY UNDER THE PRESIDENCY OF DUTCH AND GERMAN PUPPET KINGS.

1688-1885.—Thus did the "nobility, gentry, and clergy," who rose in defence of "the privileges and properties which had descended to them from their ancestors," substitute in the sacred name of liberty an oligarchical for a kingly tyranny. And this usurpation of power by the aristocracy, with the transference of the crown to nominal and alien kings, inaugurated that wanton and bloody era of English intervention in continental warfare, which was indispensable to the maintenance of a system of government destitute alike of legitimate and popular right. And this atrocious policy was omnipotent from 1688 until 1815, during one-half of which period of time England was bleeding at every pore, combating stolidly and blindly, " paying all and fighting all," as her allies jestingly observed during the disastrous War of the Austrian Succession, at the behest and in the interest of a caste and court, which ruled, injured, and deluded her. Happily, this policy received its *coup de grâce* at the hands of Mr. Disraeli, when under popular pressure— guided, sustained, and enforced by John Bright—the late remarkable Lord Beaconsfield, in gross violation of the principles of his party, took his famous " leap in the dark," or, in other words, when he virtually transferred the government of this country from the nobility, clergy, and gentry to the host of electors he called into existence. Perceiving, when too late, the momentous consequences which must inevitably flow from his revolutionary but involuntary act, he strove—after covering England with ridicule, by placing on the head of its monarch that fool's cap and bells, an Asiatic Imperial crown, and deluging Turkey with blood by the hypocrisy and imbecility of his state-craft—he as persistently as frantically strove to revive the hideous policy of the past by plunging this nation into a mad and iniquitous war in defence of Austrian and German interests, in order to divert the mind of the country from home affairs, and so to retain in the hands of the privileged classes that complete and absolute control of the reins of government which has been from time immemorial their exclusive and unchallenged birthright.

To recapitulate. The astute and ambitious Dutch Stadtholder who effected the Revolution of 1688 was as King of England—in a military sense at least—but an inglorious Edward III. or Henry V., who disastrously revived, after two centuries and a half of almost uninterrupted peace, the national animosities of England and France. Indifferent to the honour and interests of this country, he recklessly sacrificed her blood and treasure in defence of Holland. And the Dutch and their allies, who a few years previously had stemmed the tide of French conquest at Seneffe, at St. Omer, and at St. Denis, beholding in England their quixotic champion, naturally became lukewarm in their own cause, and sluggishly supported their new ally in fighting their own battles. "Let us see what sport these English bulldogs will make!" exclaimed Count Solmes derisively, as, deaf to their cries for succour, he witnessed the slaughter of Mackay and his men at the bloody fight of Steinkirk. In a word, William III. and the caste which crowned him initiated a system of foreign policy which, under this Dutch King and his German successors— and with one memorable exception in Dutch and German wars—had whitened a hundred battle-fields with the bones of Englishmen, whose every epitaph might be: "Died Abner as a fool dieth"—a policy, which rending the English race and empire in twain, has lost us the New World, and called into existence the only nation that can ever be our dangerous rival—a nation whose embattled hosts in civil strife numbered two million English-speaking combatants. Finally a policy whose simple history, illustrated with such disastrous and wanton butcheries as Landen and Malplaquet, Fontenoy and Lauffeld, Saratoga and Yorktown, is at once the most terrible indictment and strongest condemnation of that caste and alien Court which, usurping sovereign power, maintained their usurpation in the life-blood of a confiding and ingenuous people, whose interests they betrayed, whose character they belied, and whose empire they dismembered. And such is "the old traditional foreign policy" which some of our statesmen are still proud to perpetuate.

And the home policy of the nobility, clergy, and gentry was as atrocious as their foreign policy. Let us select a single incident from several of a tragic sort recorded by Smollet as an illustration of its ferocity (A.D. 1714). "One Bournois, a schoolmaster, who affirmed that King George had no right to the crown, was tried and scourged through the city, with such severity, that in a few days he expired in the utmost torture." One more fact, and I have done. (19th June, 1720.) "John Matthews, aged about eighteen, was this day executed at Tyburn, for, while an apprentice, publishing a political work." Indeed, in order to inspire an universal terror of their usurpation and tyranny, they enacted a code of English laws of the most barbarous and bloody character. On our statute-book they dared inscribe some three hundred offences, great and small—from the stealing of five shillings out of a shop, to crimes of the first magnitude—to all of which they attached the awful penalty of death. And everywhere throughout the length and breadth of the land, the gallows creaked and groaned with the dangling corpses of the unhappy victims of what the caste called " law and order."

And what was the character of our parliamentary representation under this odious domination? The control of the House of Lords and of our untitled territorial magnates —extensive owners of what were cynically called rotten, close, and pocket boroughs, which they bought and sold like other marketable property, and many of which had but a nominal existence—over the Lower House, was absolute and complete until the Reform Bill of 1832. The Duke of Norfolk was represented in the House of Commons by eleven members; Lord Lonsdale by nine; Lord Darlington by seven; the Duke of Rutland, the Marquis of Buckingham, and Lord Carrington each by six; while the families of Ponsonby, Hill, and Beresford returned sixty members to the Irish Parliament. In short, in England and Wales eighty-seven peers returned two hundred and eighteen members of parliament, and one hundred and thirty-seven more were elected by ninety commoners, and sixteen by the Government. In Scotland thirty-one of its forty-five members were chosen by twenty-one peers, and the remainder by fourteen commoners. While of the one hundred representatives of Ireland, fifty-one were sent to the second branch of the legislature by thirty-six peers, and twenty by nineteen commoners. Thus it appears that of the six hundred and fifty-eight members of the House, four hundred and eighty-seven were elected by nomination, and only one hundred and seventy-one by independent constituencies. But even in these so-called independent constituencies, the suffrage was generally so excessively narrow and unequal—at the time of the American War of Independence there were but one hundred and sixty thousand electors in England, while Scotland and Ireland had practically none at all—that their representation also, by means of unstinted bribery, coercion, and corruption, was virtually in the hands of the great neighbouring landowners. Nay, more, even in the very few great cities and commercial towns, whose voters could not be bribed, coerced, or corrupted, either by the landowners or the Government, the popular candidate, with a majority of votes, was often if not invariably prevented by the vilest of practices from securing his seat. The late Lord Farnborough assures us that, "If not defeated at the poll by riots or open violence—or defrauded of his votes by the partiality of the returning officer, or the factious manœuvres of his opponents—he was ruined by the extravagant cost of his victory. The poll was liable to be kept open for forty days, entailing an enormous expense upon the candidates, and prolific of bribery, treating, and riots. During this period, the public-houses were thrown open, and drunkenness and disorder prevailed in the streets and at the hustings. Bands of hired ruffians—armed with bludgeons, and inflamed with drink—paraded the public thoroughfares, intimidating voters, and resisting their access to the polling-places. Candidates, assailed with offensive and often dangerous missiles, braved the penalties of the pillory, while their supporters were exposed to the fury of a drunken mob." Indeed, at every period of our history—if we except the glorious era of the Long Parliament—the House of Commons represented the descendants of our conquering Norman aristocracy, and not the conquered populations of the British Isles. Well might the younger Pitt indignantly exclaim—in even too great amplitude of phrase—on seeing his strenuous efforts at political reform baffled by a coalition of the Whig and Tory sections of what was ever practically the one and indivisible ruling caste, " This House is not the representative of the people of Great Britain. It is the representative of nominal boroughs, of ruined and exterminated towns, of noble families, of wealthy individuals, of foreign potentates." And such was the monstrous parliamentary hydra which enthroned itself in 1688, on the ruins alike of the Republic and of the legitimate Monarchy.

Still, the accession of William III. gave a great impetus to the development of Puritanism, or rather to the sects to which it gave birth, and which Anglicanism has somewhat superciliously styled the Dissenting bodies. Although they had been politically crushed, owing to internal dissensions and the secession from their ranks of the Puritan nobility and gentry on the death of Cromwell, the various sects increased in numbers daily; and the accession of the Dutch Stadtholder—who was a professed Calvinist, and an advocate, not only of religious toleration, but also of the political equality of all sects—gave some degree of importance to a large section of the community, perhaps the largest numerically, which, before and since the Commonwealth, had been relentlessly persecuted by the governing powers.

In Scotland popular indignation at once swept away episcopacy, which for a quarter of a century had literally desolated that land with fire and sword.

The Anglican *régime*, under the pressure of necessity, now for the first time in its history ungraciously conceded to Dissenters' religious toleration; not, it was kind enough to inform them, as a right, but as an indulgence. The Dutch William desired that all classes of the community should participate in the government of the country, but his masters ruled otherwise. The caste decided to brand for ever as political pariahs its late conquerors; and in subsequent years it persistently strove to revoke the trifling concessions which had been wrung from it at the Glorious Revolution. Anglicanism continued to manifest the same evil, persecuting, intolerant spirit, which was inherent in the institution; and it even succeeded, in the reign of Queen Anne, in passing the iniquitous Occasional Conformity and Schism Bills, which again for a brief space crushed Dissent beneath the iron heel of persecution. But from 1719, when these Acts were repealed, a certain restricted and insolent toleration was extended to all religious bodies, save the Papists. Henceforth in large towns Dissenters could assemble together for the worship of God without fear of molestation; but in the rural districts they were still subject to the grossest outrages. There the Church, in league with ignorance, abetted and encouraged the mob in acts of violence; so that small assemblages of Dissenters were constantly liable to dispersion and brutal maltreatment. Moreover, they were debarred from serving their country in any but a menial capacity, for the cabinet, the field, the bar— in a word, every office of power, trust, and emolument was in the hands of Churchmen, and was esteemed an inheritance to which they had an inalienable and prescriptive right.

Conscious that no Stuart Prince would tolerate their monstrous usurpation of all power, or pardon their infamous betrayal of the nation and King James, the nobility, clergy, and gentry supplemented the "Glorious Revolution" of 1688 by the Act of Settlement of 1701, which, on the false pretences of liberty and religion, excluded from sovereign power the legitimate successors of the Conqueror, branding the famous Fitz Alans forsooth as mere Pretenders, and instituted the so-called Protestant succession by raising to the English throne those caricatures of royalty, our buckram Kings of the House of Hanover; the best of whom, in striving to subdue, with German serfs, the democratic offspring of the English founders of America, divided by a sea of blood the two great branches of our glorious race. Coarse, illiterate, and debauched, the heathen Welfs of the Hanoverian line stand out—bloodstained, yet ridiculous—from the pages of our history, pilloried for ever by their political crimes and social vices.

1714-1885.—In spite of the forced indulgence extended to Dissenters, the disastrous and bloody era of the Welfs was in many respects one of the darkest epochs in the history of Anglicanism. And in no respect does it appear more ominous and dark than when viewed in its educational aspect. It will be suggestive as well as instructive to mark the striking contrast presented by Puritanism and Anglicanism in the matter of universal education. It is one of the distinguishing characteristics respectively of the Norman domination symbolized by Anglicanism, and of the proper democracy of England signalized by Dissent. Unlike the Puritans—who immediately after their arrival in America initiated their famous system of free schools, which at once brought instruction to every soul of the community—the Anglican Church ever strove to paralyze the energies and stifle the nobler aspirations of the people by systematically withholding from them the inestimable boon of mental culture. Knowing its own history, and the object and end of its existence, it justly deemed ignorance its staunchest ally and surest safeguard; and naturally regarded the masses—the many-headed beast it has been the fashion to call them—as an enemy to be distrusted and depressed, rather than a friend to be enlightened and elevated. Wise in its day and generation, it consistently sealed the book of knowledge from the gaze of the multitude; for it was perfectly conscious that a modicum of mental culture, sufficient to have enabled them to appreciate a round, unvarnished history of the origin and development of Anglicanism, would have alone alienated from it the sympathies of all men whom social prejudices had not enlisted in its service, or whose personal or political interests were not bound up with its existence. And such has ever been this Church's repugnance to universal education and its cupidity, that it has not hesitated to appropriate to its own uses the ample revenues which benevolent men for many ages had bequeathed to their country, with the express object of promoting the spread of popular education. The private endowments of grammar and other charity schools which had been entrusted to its guardianship were found, even in our own times, to have been diverted from the noble object of their foundation—in a word, to have been embezzled by their spiritual administrators.

The political aspect of Anglicanism during the same epoch must be depicted in equally sombre colours. True to its own interests, and to the interests of its masters, who feared that a prolonged peace, by inducing a popular examination of home policy, might endanger their monopoly of political and sacerdotal power, this Church sanctioned with its high authority, when it did not actively encourage, those wanton and iniquitous wars which during the Georgian era dismembered our glorious empire, decimated its people, overwhelmed it with debt, and at one period menaced it with total ruin. The devoted slave of the oligarchy and of its creature, an alien Court, this Church could rank amongst its great but not disinterested patrons the German mistresses of our German kings. And yet the second George—ungrateful to the caste which permitted him to wage on German soil, with British troops, for fifteen years, two bloody and inglorious wars with France—was especially fond of reviling his sycophantic partisans, the prelates of the Church of which he was the supreme temporal head. For example, when Sherlock, Bishop of Salisbury, wrote against the Quakers' Relief Bill, our coarse and dissolute Defender of the Faith described the Fathers of the Church as "a parcel of black-coated, canting, hypocritical rascals." And to the remonstrances of his Queen, who desired him to be less severe in his strictures on the bishops, this royal punchinello—steeped to the lips in British blood—is reported to have replied, "I am sick to death of all this foolish stuff, and wish with all my heart that the devil may take all your bishops, and the devil take your minister, and the devil take the Parliament, and the devil take the whole Island, provided I can get out of it and go to

Hanover." But notwithstanding this petulant outburst of royal sentiment, the foreign king was powerless to harm the Church, which had now attained the summit of its material prosperity. It was in possession of one-twelfth of the revenue of England, yet the dignitaries of that Church, the priests who officiated at her altars, the spiritual shepherds of the poor and infirm of a suffering nation, were—I speak advisedly—amongst the most unprincipled of mankind. When, in addition to this charge, I assert without fear of contradiction, that hypocrisy, that simony, that infidelity, stalked unabashed through every grade of that time-serving priesthood, I have painted a picture of sacerdotal iniquity to which the whole world scarcely affords a parallel.

Such were the antecedents of Anglicanism until 1828, when the Test and Corporations Acts were repealed, and the Catholic Emancipation Bill was passed in the teeth of its opposition. Then were the Dissenters completely freed from the Anglican yoke, from a tyranny over the conscience unexampled for its duration and cold-blooded ferocity. But the artificial and unjust distinctions and privileges of a religious caste still remain to perpetuate and enforce, though less ostentatiously than of yore, the arrogance and political traditions of Anglicanism, and to create an impassable gulf between the co-religionists of Milton and Cromwell, and the disciples of Laud and Charles I.; or rather between the democracy of England, and the ancient Norman domination, of which Anglicanism was the offspring, and has ever been the spiritual representative and champion.

At first sight it appears somewhat singular that Englishmen who are ordinarily so jealous of the renown of their compatriots, should suffer the deeds of the Pilgrims to perish in oblivion, and that they should tolerate the malignity of the calumniators, who have systematically vilified the heroes of the Commonwealth. But the strangeness of this neglect and ingratitude is apparent rather than real when we reflect that the Anglican Church—together with the ancient Norman domination—the persecutor of the Pilgrims, the vanquished, but, in the very nature of things, the eternal enemy of its Puritan destroyers—is still, in name at least, triumphant in our midst. That this Church, besides being in the enjoyment of fabulous revenues, is the main, I had almost said, the only avenue to all preferment, and that moreover retaining almost exclusive possession of the universities and all public educational endowments, it is not only in a position to bribe, coerce, or crush the trained intellect of the country, but is also enabled to mould the mind of that section of the community which has hitherto governed us at its will. That being a political rather than a religious organization, it regards events from a purely professional and secular standpoint, and impregnates all its instruction with an Anglican, that is to say, an anti-Puritan leaven, ever making its artificial Christianity subservient to its political aims. Finally, that being imbued with the principle which gave it existence, and which constitutes its present vitality, this Church believes self-interest to be the cardinal and invariable motor of mankind, and is therefore incapable of appreciating the stern self-sacrificing faith of the Puritans, whose motives it misrepresents, whose reputation it slanders, and whose achievements it ignores.

And when, in our own day, the prelates of this institution, with real or affected ignorance, make arrogant and insolent allusions to what they are pleased to call Dissent, it is time that the descendants of the Puritans should remind their persecutors that we, in common with our glorious ancestors, repel their institution, not as a religious sect, but as a political and anti-national organization, created and subsidized by despotic monarchs, and subsequently sustained by the governing oligarchical caste for the maintenance and perpetuity of their respective tyrannies. We charge them with having, in return for a lavish bestowal of honours and wealth, systematically prostituted the Word of God itself to the political purposes of their royal and noble patrons. And in common with the " Pilgrims," we denounce their ceremonies and dignities as " monuments of idolatry," and deem the Scriptures in their hands as " holy things in the custody of the profane, the Ark of the Lord in the hands of the Philistines." We are conscious that, but for disunion and culpable lukewarmness in the ranks of Dissent, the existence of their monstrous institution to our own times had been impossible—in spite of its Jesuitical organization, its boundless wealth, and its political connections. But, notwithstanding our shortcomings and our derelictions of duty in the cause of political truth, we believe we see the beginning of the end of Anglicanism, which success alone has rendered respectable and tolerable, and which will fall, like its parent stem of Rome and its rejeton of Ireland, amidst the execrations and contempt of mankind. And with its destruction we shall witness the complete triumph of the glorious principles of independent Christian worship and national sovereignty in combating which Anglicanism has sacrificed hecatombs of victims.

Happily the political system, founded in blood and rapine by the Norman Duke—which since 1688 had degenerated into a vast and permanent combination against the British nation of the aristocracy and Church, headed by their Dutch and German puppet kings—has been shattered to pieces by legislative victories more glorious and enduring than Marston Moor and Naseby. And its destruction must speedily entail the dissolution and final disappearance of the Conqueror's throne. Then will for ever cease that fatal influence which our German Court has exercised since 1714 over the foreign policy of England, an influence which in the past lost us America and made us the cheap defence of Germany against the French, and which in the future might possibly involve us still in the interests of Germany in perpetual rivalry or hostility with her natural and dreaded enemy Russia, twenty millions of whose race the Germans and Austro-Germans hold in brutal bondage.

Meanwhile, it will be well to remind the prelates that the descendants of the Puritans have a history as well as they, but a history free from the brand of persecution and the taint of State patronage. The co-religionists of the Protector Cromwell, of Hampden and Blake, of Milton and Bunyan, of Vane and Penn, and of a host of good as well as great men, have nothing to desire in the matter of mere earthly renown. To their galaxy of illustrious dead it would be difficult to find in the world's annals worthy parallels. The brightest page of England's history is but a record of their achievements. Subverting the ancient Norman domination, which for centuries had oppressed her, the Puritans, by their genius and valour, made Republican England the terror and wonder of the world. And their persecuted ones, "whom nothing but the wide ocean and the savage deserts of America could hide and shelter from the fury of the bishops," have increased and multiplied until they have become a great nation, perhaps at this moment the greatest nation on earth, at whose whisper the throne of Maximilian vanished into thin air, and his body mouldered into dust; at whose command the legions of France slunk, with hurried and fearful tread, from American soil; the moral effects of whose might withered the laurels of Solferino and the Malakoff, and shook to its very centre the throne of the late crowned conspirator of the Tuileries.

Whilst I lament the narrow-minded obstinacy of an alien king, and the tyrannical and illegal acts of an oligarchy which destroyed the unity of the English-speaking race, and cost us the most desirable land the sun looks down upon, I rejoice none the less in its prosperity and might, for I cannot forget that its people have sprung from our own loins, that they

> "Speak the tongue
> That Shakespeare spoke—the faith and morals hold
> Which Milton held;"

and that in spite of passing clouds and jarring interests which the foreign element in America embitters, envenoms, and often creates, I firmly believe—and I speak with a personal knowledge of the country—that the heart of the native born American nation is as our heart; and that the nightly prayer of the first American colonists, " God bless England, our dear native land," finds to-day a responsive echo in every Anglo-American breast. I believe that the still small English voice which guides and controls the destinies of the Great Republic will at all times silence the clamours of its naturalized but alien citizens, and allay the quickly irritated susceptibilities of its own people; and that all the clouds which may lower upon the kindred nations will be " in the deep bosom of the ocean buried." Finally, I believe that the sound, unfettered, English common-sense of both countries will eventually restore that unity to the English-speaking race which the political crimes of an oligarchy destroyed, and that England—with her mighty brood of nascent giant nations—and America, marching hand-in-hand in the forefront of civilization, will raise regenerate and free the poor and oppressed masses of mankind.

THE END.

www.ingramcontent.com/pod-product-compliance
Lightning Source LLC
Chambersburg PA
CBHW021158230426
43667CB00006B/460